From that first cup of tea or coffe[e]
bowl of porridge we start our day
spaghetti with tomato sauce or s[ome]
rice we eat for supper, the kitche[n]
with plants in a very special way.
us. Human beings have long eaten and enjoyed greens,
spices, grains, pulses, roots, fungi and fruit.

This cookbook celebrates both the glorious variety of
edible plants and fungi that we eat and the vital work
that the Royal Botanic Gardens, Kew does to promote and
sustain this rich biodiversity. All the recipes have been
generously donated by wonderful chefs and food writers
to support Kew. The theme of coming together reflected
by the contributors to this book is important. Sharing
food is a special way of connecting with others; it is at the
heart of hospitality. Taking the time and trouble to cook
for others is nourishing in so many ways. In our hectic
world, the time spent together over meals – with the
chance to talk and share our thoughts and feelings – is
precious. If changing how we eat can help our beautiful,
precious planet, then surely we need to embrace that.
These are challenging times for the Earth and we humans
need to unite to look after it.

THE
KEW GARDENS
COOKBOOK

THE
KEW GARDENS
COOKBOOK

A CELEBRATION OF PLANTS IN THE KITCHEN

67 vegetarian recipes from leading chefs and food writers

Edited by Jenny Linford

Photography by Hugh Johnson

Kew Publishing
Royal Botanic Gardens Kew

Contents

Introduction

From that first cup of tea or coffee and slice of toast or bowl of muesli or porridge we start our day with, to the bowl of spaghetti with tomato sauce or stir-fried vegetables with rice we eat for supper, the kitchen is where we connect with plants in a very special way. They literally sustain us. This vegetarian cookbook celebrates both the glorious variety of edible plants and fungi that we eat and the vital work that the Royal Botanic Gardens, Kew does to promote and sustain the rich biodiversity of the plant and fungi world.

Plants have long formed an important part of the human diet and they have played a fundamental role in our history. Our hunter-gatherer ancestors foraged in the wild for fruits, roots, leaves and seeds. In an important stage in human development around 11,000 years ago, at the origins of agriculture, humans started farming cereal, legume and root crops and began a worldwide shift from being hunter gathers to farmers. The growing of food crops and the rise of farming are key to the subsequent development of towns, cities and civilizations. To this day, plant foods continue to be central to our diets around the world. According to the United Nations' Food and Agriculture Organization, while there are over 50,000 edible plants in the world, just 15 crop plants provide 90 per cent of the world's food energy intake, with three key crops – rice, maize and wheat – providing 60 per cent of that intake.

We increasingly understand how important eating plants is for our health. Plants are rich in antioxidants, which our bodies need to maintain good health, and are an important source of both vitamins and fibre. Importantly, there is also the health of the planet to consider. In a time of climate change and population growth, the quest for a sustainable diet is a crucial one. It is widely agreed that in order to slow climate warming, one important thing we can all do as individuals is reduce our meat consumption and eat more plants. Interestingly, a recent Oxford University study advises that increasing our consumption of whole grain cereals, fruits, vegetables, nuts and legumes would benefit both human health and the environment. Summing up what he had learnt about food and health, the American food writer Michael Pollan gave his advice concisely: 'eat food, not too much, mostly plants'.

Climate change and its impact on the plants we depend on to sustain life is an issue which Kew takes very seriously. Central to Kew's work is a fight against biodiversity loss. One important strand of this is preserving genetic diversity. Soberingly, two in five plant species are in danger of extinction. Kew's Millennium Seed Bank at Wakehurst, Kew's wild botanic garden in Sussex, stores over 2.4 billion seeds from around the world to conserve them for the future. Among these saved seeds are the wild cousins of our food crops. Over time, through selective breeding, many commercially grown crops have lost genetic diversity and resilience. The hope is that the conserved crop wild relatives have characteristics that could be useful in developing new varieties that are more resilient to climate change.

Climate change threatens to bring with it new weather conditions, plant pests and diseases that our existing food crops will struggle to cope with. With the world's human population growing, maintaining food security is an issue that needs addressing urgently. Kew is carrying out important research to help identify potential future foods, such as the morama bean, fonio and enset, which could be key sustainable crops to feed a hungry world.

All the recipes in this cookbook have been kindly donated by wonderful chefs and food writers – including Raymond Blanc, Diana Henry, Thomasina Miers, Yotam Ottolenghi and Claudia Roden, to name but a few – in order to help Kew continue its important research. As you will see looking through this book, there is a joyful diversity to the recipes within its pages. A wide variety of fruits, nuts, vegetables, pulses, grains and fungi are used in dishes that range from simple, comforting suppers – ideal for a midweek meal after a busy day – to glorious cakes with which to celebrate birthdays and other special occasions. Vietnamese summer rolls, Indian curries and street food snacks, a classic French gratin, an English suet pudding . . . our contributors have shared recipes drawn from cuisines around the world. It is easy to get stuck in a rut with one's cooking. One of the aims of this cookbook is to offer inspiration when it comes to cooking with plants. Human beings are an ingenious species and I feel that is well expressed in the way in which we cook with plants. From the herbs and spices which add an intense burst of flavour, to leaves used as edible wrappers, roots and grains added to cakes and tarts, and flower petals used to add fragrance to a fruit-based jelly, *The Kew Gardens Cookbook* is full of ideas for how to enjoy cooking with and eating plants and fungi.

The theme of coming together – reflected by the generosity of the contributors to this cookbook – is important. Sharing food is a special way of connecting with others; it is at the heart of hospitality. Taking the time and trouble to cook for others is nourishing in so many ways. In our hectic world, the time spent together over meals – with the chance to talk and share our thoughts and feelings – is precious. If changing how we eat can help our beautiful, precious planet, then surely we need to embrace that. These are challenging times for the Earth and we humans need to unite to look after it.

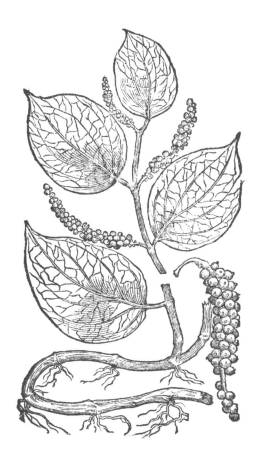

The Royal Botanic Gardens, Kew

The Royal Botanic Gardens, Kew is a world-famous scientific organisation, internationally respected for its outstanding collections as well as its expertise in plant and fungal diversity, conservation, and scientific development. Such is its significance, in 2003 Kew Gardens was inscribed as a UNESCO World Heritage Site. Kew's landscaped gardens and Wakehurst, Kew's wild botanic garden in Sussex, attract over 2.5 million visitors a year. At its 320-acre site in London, Kew Gardens is home to 16,900 species of plants from all over the world and holds the Guinness World Record for being the 'largest collection of living plants at a single-site botanic garden.'

Kew's origins date back to 1759, when Princess Augusta, mother of King George III, founded a nine-acre botanic garden within the pleasure grounds at Kew Palace. The 18th century was an age of scientific curiosity, exploration and imperial expansion, and this is reflected in the way the botanic garden at Kew developed and expanded. Exciting new plants were collected from around the world and showcased in the Royal Botanic Gardens. The noted naturalist Joseph Banks sent seeds to Kew in 1768 while on Captain Cook's expedition to the South Pacific, and on his return became Kew Gardens' first unofficial director. Banks instigated an overseas plant collecting programme; under his guidance Kew's collection of plants expanded considerably, and botanical research began.

In 1840 responsibility for Kew transferred from the Crown to the government. William Jackson Hooker was appointed its first official director and the Gardens were opened to the public. The striking Palm House (completed in 1848) and Temperate House (which opened in 1863) were constructed using innovative Victorian technology and remain iconic Kew buildings to this day.

From its start, collecting plants has been central to Kew's purpose and these Living Collections are a unique and important research resource. Kew's Herbarium was built in 1853; today it houses around seven million preserved vascular plant specimens, offering a wealth of information about plants that have been amassed over the past 170 years. The scale and range of Kew's collections is striking. Kew has one of the largest collections of botanical literature, art, and archive material in the world. Kew's Millennium Seed Bank (MSB) at Wakehurst opened in 2000 and is the largest wild plant seed bank in the world. As the planet faces a biodiversity crisis, with two-fifths of the world's plants in danger of extinction, the MSB, along with its global partners, are vital to keeping vulnerable and economically important plants safe. While the Norwegian seed bank Svalbard stores seeds of the world's crops, the MSB banks wild plants, including seeds from about 400 crop wild relative species. These seeds have a crucial part to play in sustaining biodiversity.

Long at the forefront of global plant and fungal research, Kew's mission is to understand and protect plants and fungi, for the wellbeing of people and the future of all life on earth. Plants and fungi are vital for the future of food, the air we breathe, and medicine. In a time of extinction and climate crisis, Kew's work has never been more vital or more urgent.

Inside the Palm House

Kitchen gardens at Kew

The kitchen gardens at Kew are a beautiful example of the aesthetic – as well as culinary – pleasures of growing edible fruits and vegetables. When the original nine-acre botanic garden at Kew was founded in 1759, a large and impressive kitchen garden covering an area of 12 acres existed within the pleasure grounds at Kew. The garden needed to be on this scale as it catered for the royal households of Princess Augusta and George III and their servants when they stayed at Kew, and it could supply the household anywhere within a 20-mile radius. In order to supply fashionable and exotic fruits for the royal households, the Kew kitchen garden included seven peach houses, two vineries, two cherry houses, three pineapple stoves plus a range of pineapple pits and a mushroom house. Melons were grown in an area that is still known today as the Melon Yard. In 1810, William Townsend Aiton, Kew's head gardener, produced more than 200 baskets of forced figs for the royal table and, therefore, felt able to request an increase of £100 in funding for the gardens. In the 1840s, however, after new kitchen gardens had been laid out at Windsor Castle, the royal kitchen gardens at Kew were disbanded.

Food crops were, however, grown at Kew during both world wars as part of the drive to help make Britain self-sufficient. During the Second World War, when supplies of seed potatoes could not meet demand, Kew was approached by the Ministry of Food to provide a solution. William Campbell, Kew's curator, discovered that potatoes could be cultivated by using slices of the tuber instead of the whole tuber, as long as the slices contained an 'eye', which dramatically increased supply. During the 'Dig for Victory' campaign, Kew provided training on cultivating food crops, made land available for local residents, and created 'model' allotments tended to by women gardeners to instruct the public on the best way to grow their own vegetables.

In 2014, a new kitchen garden was created at Kew on the same site as the original royal kitchen gardens. One of the aims of the restored kitchen garden is to reinforce the links between Kew's research into plant diversity, chemistry and genetics and the hands-on, day-to-day growing of our food. This carefully tended, productive space, filled with edible plants, seeks to inspire people to discover the fundamental pleasures of planting, growing and harvesting. The planting in the kitchen garden reflects Kew's focus on maintaining food security in an age of climate change. So, for example, Hélèna Dove, Kew's kitchen gardener, experimented with less familiar root crops. The best results came from oca (*Oxalis tuberosa*) and mashua (*Tropaeolum tuberosum*) which grew well and had the highest yield. While like the potato (*Solanum tuberosum*) these plants originate from the Andes, unlike the potato they are not affected by blight, which can destroy entire potato crops. This resilience makes them an important potential future food.

Tomatoes growing in the
Kew kitchen garden

The Palm House

Yotam Ottolenghi
Tomato and ricotta salad with coriander seed and lemon oil

Jill Norman
Spiced pumpkin soup

Fuchsia Dunlop
Fish-fragrant aubergines: *yuxiang qiezi*

Angela Clutton
Rhubarb upside-down cake with blood orange
and cardamom curd

 # HERBS AND SPICES

Mark Diacono
Three herb spelt with cucumber and pomegranate

Asma Khan
Spiced aubergine in garlic raita: *dahi baingan*

Kathy Slack
Pumpkin and sage cake with thyme and feta frosting

Ken Hom
Thai-inspired mixed vegetable salad

Özlem Warren
Baked cauliflower with red onions, feta and dill:
firinda karnabahar mucveri

The herbs and spices which we use to add flavour and fragrance to our food come from plants. Their contribution to culinary pleasure is quite remarkable, especially so when one considers the small quantities often used. It is quite extraordinary how much aroma adding just one bay leaf, a bruised stalk of lemon grass, a few curry leaves, a pinch of saffron will give to a dish. One only has to pause and try to imagine cooking without garlic, ginger, chillies, vanilla or mint to realise how much less enjoyable and interesting our food would be if we didn't use herbs and spices. No wonder that every cuisine around the world uses herbs and spices to enhance their food.

The word herb has its origins in the Latin *herba*, meaning grass or green crop. Culinary herbs are the leaves or stems of plants, used fresh or dried. It is important to use fresh herbs quickly as their volatile aromas dissipate very fast; often they are torn or chopped and added to dishes at the last minute. Different methods are used to extract flavour from herbs. Herbs with tougher leaves, such as rosemary, bay or thyme – are added to stews and braises or inserted into meat to be roasted. Some recipes call for herbs to be pounded to release their aromas, as with Thai green curry paste – flavoured with fresh coriander – or Italy's pesto Genovese made using fresh basil, both traditionally made using mortar and pestles, though nowadays people often use food processors. In other recipes, herbs add their flavour through infusion in a liquid, as with French cookery where a bouquet garni (classically parsley, thyme and bay) is used to flavour stock and sauces, while in South-East Asia a knotted pandan leaf adds its subtle grassy flavour to a palm sugar syrup. Herb teas or tisanes are made by steeping fresh or dried leaves – such as mint or lemon verbena – in water.

One of the pleasures of herbs is that many of them can be successfully grown in pots on a windowsill, balcony, patio or in a garden, allowing the home cook ready access to freshly picked herbs. Growing your own herbs also allows you to expand your herb range by growing herbs which are less widely available in food shops, such as lemon verbena, chervil (with its delicate anise notes), lovage and Vietnamese coriander.

Spices often consist of seeds, buds, herbs, roots and fruits, usually but not always dried, and are used both whole and ground into powders. Nowadays in Britain we take spices for granted as an everyday kitchen store-cupboard ingredient, but centuries ago they were a costly luxury, imported from countries far away, prized for both the way they flavoured food and their preserving properties. Their value and the fact that they were small, light and highly portable, meant that dried spices lent themselves to trading, and numerous spice trade routes were created across the globe. The search for valuable spices, such as clove and nutmeg, and the quest for lucrative trading routes motivated European countries, such as Portugal, Holland, Britain and Spain, to travel to and colonise countries around the globe. Colonisation and trade saw many spices spread through the world outside the countries where they originally came from. Chillies, for instance, now play a key part in Indian cuisine, yet the chilli plant was not indigenous to India. Chillies are believed to have come originally from Bolivia, with Mexico the first country to have cultivated chillies. It is thought that the Portuguese introduced chillies to India in the 15th century via Goa.

When it comes to cooking with spices, there are simple ways to maximise their flavour. Spices deteriorate over time, so buy small quantities and store them in airtight containers in a cool, dark cupboard or drawer. Dry-roasting spices, such as cumin seeds – done by heating them for a few minutes in a frying pan with no oil – enhances and deepens their flavour and also makes them easier to grind. One of the interesting things about spices in the kitchen is the way that they are often combined with each other to make spice mixtures, like Bengali panch phoran (five spice mixture), Ethiopia's berbere and China's five spice powder. As well as using these classic combinations, there is much scope to make your own spice mixtures to use as marinade rubs or to flavour curries.

Herbs and spices have long been highly valued for their medicinal uses as well as their culinary ones, playing an important part, for example, in both Chinese and Indian traditional medicine. It is this medicinal aspect of herbs and spices which is of particular interest to Kew. Kew has catalogued plant-based medicines (regulated drugs, traditional remedies and plants used by indigenous and rural communities) and the circa 33,000 plants from which they derive, a number of which are herbs or plants from which we derive spices. The ongoing search for new medicines often begins by exploring traditional uses of plants (ethnopharmacology), while plants in our diet may also offer potential health benefits. So, for example, with dementia on the rise around the world, Kew and its collaborators, taking inspiration from 17th- and 18th- century British herbals, are exploring how chemicals in herbs including rosemary, lemon balm and sage can affect cognitive functions such as memory.

Chillies growing in the
Kew kitchen garden

Yotam Ottolenghi

Tomato and ricotta salad with coriander seed and lemon oil

This is a celebration of summer tomatoes. Cherry tomatoes work well, because they are so sweet, but use whatever you have to hand. The dressing and oil can be made a day in advance.

Serves 8

8 plum tomatoes (750g),
cut in half

250ml olive oil

3 unpeeled garlic cloves

salt and black pepper

3 tbsp PX sherry vinegar,
or any other sweet vinegar
such as moscatel

1 lemon, 3 wide strips of zest
pared off with a peeler or sharp
knife, then squeezed, to get
2 tbsp juice

800g heritage cherry tomatoes

20g picked basil leaves,
roughly chopped

70g spring onions, trimmed
and thinly sliced at an angle

100g ricotta dura (hard ricotta),
thinly sliced

For the sourdough croutons

360g sourdough bread,
crust removed, then torn into
medium chunks

60ml olive oil

For the coriander seed and lemon oil

45ml olive oil

3 strips lemon zest

1½ tbsp coriander seeds,
lightly crushed

Heat the oven to its highest setting – 240ºC/220ºC fan. Put the plum tomatoes skin side down in a roughly 23cm x 17cm x 7cm high ovenproof dish, then add the oil, whole garlic cloves and a teaspoon of salt. Roast for 25 minutes, until the tomato juices are running and the skins are blistered, then remove and leave to cool. Turn down the oven to 180ºC/160ºC fan.

Once cool, peel and discard both the tomato and garlic skins, then, using a fork, mash them into the oily juices in the dish until completely broken up. Add 2 tbsp of the sherry vinegar and the lemon juice, stir well and put to one side.

In a colander set over a bowl, mix the cherry tomatoes with a ½ tsp salt and the remaining tablespoon of vinegar and set aside to steep.

Put the chunks of sourdough on a large baking tray, drizzle over the olive oil, toss to coat, then bake for about 25 minutes, until golden and crunchy. Remove and leave to cool.

Meanwhile, make the coriander seed oil by heating the olive oil and lemon zest in a small frying pan on medium heat for about 2 minutes. Add the coriander seeds, cook for another minute, until they become fragrant, then take off the heat and leave to cool.

To assemble, spoon the dressing on to a large platter, scatter the croutons on top, then scatter over half the basil, spring onions and ricotta. Tumble the cherry tomatoes on top with the remaining basil, spring onions and ricotta, drizzle over the coriander oil and serve.

Jill Norman
Spiced pumpkin soup

Once you've cleaned the pumpkin, this soup is fast to make. Pumpkin's mild, sweet taste combines well with coconut milk, and both are enhanced by the spices. In this soup, the citrus flavours of lemon grass and coriander set off the bite of ginger and chillies, with a background note of earthy turmeric.

Vegan
Serves 4–6

2 tbsp sunflower oil

½ tsp coriander seeds

1 tsp turmeric

1 large onion, chopped

2cm piece of fresh root ginger, chopped

2 garlic cloves, chopped

1kg pumpkin, peeled, deseeded and cubed

2 dried chillies

2 stalks lemon grass, bruised

Salt to taste

600ml vegetable stock

400ml coconut milk

lime juice (optional)

country bread, to serve

Heat the oil in a large, heavy-based saucepan and fry the coriander and turmeric until their aromas are released. Stir in the onion, ginger and garlic, and fry for a few minutes more. Then add the pumpkin, chillies and lemon grass. Stir well, season with a little salt, and pour over the stock. Cover the pan and simmer until the pumpkin softens, then stir in the coconut milk. Don't cover the pan now, or the coconut milk may curdle.

Bring the soup back to a simmer and cook until the pumpkin is soft enough to crush with a wooden spoon. Discard the chillies and lemon grass, and blend and strain the soup.

Taste, and if you wish to sharpen the flavour, stir in a little lime juice. Serve with country bread.

Fuchsia Dunlop

Fish-fragrant aubergines: *yuxiang qiezi* 鱼香茄子

The following recipe is a local classic, and one of my all-time favourite dishes of any cuisine. More than any other dish, for me it sums up the luxuriant pleasures of Sichuanese food: the warm colours and tastes, the subtlety of complex flavours.

Like other fish-fragrant dishes, it is made with the seasonings of traditional fish cookery: pickled chillies, garlic, ginger and spring onions. But unlike the more illustrious fish-fragrant pork slivers, it derives its colour not from pickled chillies alone, but from pickled chillies combined with broad beans in chilli bean paste. The sauce is sweet, sour and spicy, with a reddish hue and a visible scattering of chopped ginger, garlic and spring onion.

The dish is equally delicious hot or cold. I usually serve it with a meat or tofu dish and a stir-fried green vegetable, but it makes a fine lunch simply eaten with brown rice and a salad. The aubergines, deep-fried to a buttery tenderness, are delectable. I have eaten this dish in restaurants all over Sichuan, and recorded numerous different versions of the recipe. The following one will, I hope, make you sigh with delight.

Vegan

600g aubergines

cooking oil, for deep-frying

1½ tbsp Sichuan chilli bean paste

1½ tbsp finely chopped garlic

1 tbsp finely chopped ginger

150ml hot stock or water

4 tsp caster sugar

1 tsp light soy sauce

¾ tsp potato starch, mixed with 1 tbsp cold water

1 tbsp Chinkiang vinegar

6 tbsp thinly sliced spring onion greens

salt

Cut the aubergines into batons about 2cm thick and 7cm long. Sprinkle with salt, mix well and set aside for at least 30 minutes.

Rinse the aubergines, drain well and pat dry with kitchen paper. Heat the deep-frying oil to around 200°C (hot enough to sizzle vigorously around a test piece of aubergine). Add the aubergines, in two or three batches, and deep-fry for about 3 minutes, until tender and a little golden. Drain well on kitchen paper and set aside.

Carefully pour off all but 3 tbsp oil from the wok and return to a medium flame. Add the chilli bean paste and stir-fry until the oil is red and fragrant: take care not to burn the paste (move the wok away from the burner if you think it might be overheating). Add the garlic and ginger and stir-fry until they smell delicious.

Tip in the stock or water, sugar and soy sauce. Bring to the boil, then add the aubergines, nudging them gently into the sauce so the pieces do not break apart. Simmer for a minute or so to allow the aubergines to absorb the flavours.

Give the potato starch mixture a stir and add it gradually, in about three stages, adding just enough to thicken the sauce to a luxurious gravy (you probably won't need it all). Tip in the vinegar and all but 1 tbsp of the spring onion greens, then stir for a few seconds to fuse the flavours.

Turn out on to a serving dish, scatter over the remaining spring onion greens and serve.

If you want to scale up this recipe for a party, rinse and dry the salted aubergines, toss in a little cooking oil and then roast for 15–20 minutes in a 220°C oven until golden. Make the sauce, but don't thicken it with starch; instead, pour it over the roasted aubergines and set aside to allow the flavours to mingle. Serve at room temperature.

Angela Clutton
Rhubarb upside-down cake with blood orange and cardamom curd

This is a heavenly cake and pleasingly pretty to boot – especially if you use the pinkest stalks of rhubarb you can get your hands on. Its joy owes a lot to the blood orange curd that is flecked with cardamom and bakes within the cake. It becomes a sort of sauce for the rhubarb, suffusing the sponge with its silky fabulousness.

For the blood orange and cardamom curd

3–4 blood oranges

80g caster sugar

1 large eggs + 2 egg yolks, beaten

80g cold butter, cut into small cubes

1 tsp cornflour

6 cardamom pods, crushed

For the cake

250g butter, softened

1 tbsp soft brown sugar

500g rhubarb, trimmed and cut into 5cm lengths

200g caster sugar

3 large eggs, beaten

240g self-raising flour

1 tsp baking powder

2 tbsp full-fat Greek yoghurt

blood orange and cardamom curd as above

1 tbsp icing sugar

To make the curd

Zest three of the oranges into a bowl and set that aside. Now halve the oranges you've zested and squeeze their juice – you're hoping for approx. 150ml. Use the fourth orange if you need to.

Sit a heatproof bowl over a pan of simmering water, ensuring the base of the bowl doesn't touch the water. Put the orange juice, sugar, eggs, butter, cornflour and cardamom into the bowl and whisk to combine. Stir continuously over the simmering water for the curd to thicken – it will take approx. 10–12 minutes from the point the butter has melted. When the curd coats the back of a spoon, turn off the heat. Lift out the cardamom pods (it's fine to leave their seeds behind), transfer the curd to a cool bowl, stir in the orange zest, and set aside to cool and thicken.

To make the cake

Preheat the oven to 180°C/160°C fan. Grease a 22cm springform cake tin and line its base.

Gently melt 10g of the butter in a saucepan, and use a pastry brush to spread over the papered base of the tin. Scatter over the soft brown sugar. Arrange the rhubarb pieces in the tin in whatever design you fancy, putting them tightly together.

Mix together the rest of butter and caster sugar until pale and fluffy. Beat in the eggs, then fold in the flour, baking powder and a pinch of salt. Add the yoghurt and mix just enough to combine. Spoon about a third of the cake batter on top of the rhubarb and spread the cold curd over that. Now dot on top the rest of the batter, and spread using the back of a spoon.

Bake for 50 minutes to an hour until springy and a skewer into the top layer of the cake comes out clean. Cool the cake in its tin for 15 minutes before gently turning over onto a wire rack so the rhubarb is uppermost. Remove the tin and paper and leave the cake to cool. Dust with icing sugar and enjoy.

Mark Diacono
Three herb spelt with cucumber and pomegranate

This is a fantastic core recipe, a version of which is in my book *Herb*. Tweak it as you please, to use whichever herbs are in season, plentiful and that you fancy. It's almost a tabbouleh: be similarly generous with the herbs.

Favourite herb combinations include: parsley, fennel, chives; coriander, mint, parsley; basil, chives, chervil; tarragon, parsley, chives; parsley, mint, lovage. This is substantial enough to with go with leafy salads or barbecued vegetables in summer, or as a side with others or a more substantial main when the weather is cooler. I like to cut the herbs into thin filaments as it gives bursts of flavour that a finer chop misses. The sharpest of knives is crucial to avoid bruising the leaves.

Vegan
Serves 4

250g pearled spelt

a very generous handful of fresh herbs

1 cucumber, diced

seeds from 2 pomegranates

zest of 1 lemon, juice of half

150ml extra virgin olive oil

salt and finely ground black pepper

Rinse the spelt thoroughly, place in a pan and cover with water. Bring to the boil, reduce to a simmer and cook until just firm: 20–25 minutes is usual. Drain in a sieve and allow to release its steam for a few minutes.

Roll all the herbs into a cigar and slice finely to give thin filaments.

Place the cucumber and pomegranate seeds in a bowl, add the lemon juice, zest, olive oil, and season well. Stir the herbs in. Add the spelt and stir to incorporate everything thoroughly.

Taste and adjust the seasonings if necessary. Serve immediately, warm.

Asma Khan
Spiced aubergine in garlic raita: *dahi baingan*

A great side dish to have with kababs and parathas, I love this combination of thinly fried aubergine slices covered in garlic raita. In fact, this is my all-time favourite raita. In my family, this garlicky yoghurt was always considered superior to the simple cucumber and tomato raita. But as *dahi baingan* was only made for important feasts, I got to enjoy its garlic raita accompaniment infrequently. Nowadays, I treat myself to this delicious dish far more often.

Serves 8

For the spiced aubergine
4 medium aubergines, thinly sliced into discs
1 tsp ground turmeric
½ tsp chilli powder
1 tsp salt
oil, for frying

For the garlic raita
500g full-fat Turkish or Greek yoghurt
6 garlic cloves, crushed
½ tsp chilli powder
1 tsp salt
½ tsp brown sugar

For the tempering
10 fresh curry leaves
3 dried red chillies, broken in half

To make the garlic raita, mix all the ingredients together in a bowl. Taste to check the seasoning and adjust as necessary. Place in a serving dish.

To make the spiced aubergines, rub the ground turmeric, chilli powder and salt into the aubergine slices. Set aside for 20 minutes. When ready to cook, squeeze the aubergine slices to remove any excess water.

Ideally, use a deep-fat fryer or, if you haven't got one, use a heavy-based saucepan over a medium–high heat to heat the oil to 180°C. Test the temperature by putting a cube of bread in the oil – if it immediately starts to crisp up then the oil is ready. Working in batches, deep-fry the aubergine slices until golden brown. Using a slotted spoon, remove from the oil and drain on a plate.

Layer the deep-fried aubergine slices on top of the garlic yoghurt in the serving dish. To make the tempering, heat 2 tbsp of the oil used to fry the aubergines in a small frying pan. Add the curry leaves and dried red chillies and cook, stirring, for 1 minute. Pour over the aubergine slices and yoghurt. Serve immediately.

Kathy Slack
Pumpkin and sage cake with thyme and feta frosting

I know this sounds a bit odd, but, really, it's just a carrot cake that took a wrong turn in life and ended up somewhere more interesting. The herbs add a floral, garden air to things and the citrus twang of feta makes the cream cheese frosting pleasingly eccentric. You can use any winter squash or pumpkin, however some varieties, usually the paler ones, can be rather watery when grated, in which case, squeeze out the water from the gratings before adding to the batter. This is a pudding-y cake, equally at home with an afternoon cuppa as it is with a chilled sweet wine for dessert.

Serves 8

300g self-raising flour

250g soft light brown sugar

2 tsp bicarbonate of soda

½ tsp flaky sea salt

200g butter, melted and slightly cooled

4 eggs

500g winter pumpkin or squash, peeled, deseeded and coarsely grated (see intro)

10 sage leaves, finely chopped

For the frosting

75g feta cheese

200g full-fat cream cheese

200ml double cream

75g runny honey

2 tbsp chopped thyme leaves, and a few edible flowers such as thyme flowers if in season

Preheat the oven to 205°C/185°C fan. Line two 20cm round cake tins with baking parchment.

Mix the flour, sugar, bicarbonate of soda and salt in a large bowl.

Whisk together the cooled melted butter and eggs in a jug. Pour into the bowl of dry ingredients and stir together. You will think, 'no good can come of this', but trust me. Add the grated pumpkin or squash and the chopped sage and mix well.

Divide the batter equally between the two lined cake tins, levelling off the top, then bake for 40 minutes or until a skewer comes out clean when inserted into the middle of the cakes.

While the cakes cook, make the buttercream frosting. Use a spatula to smudge the feta into a paste in a large bowl. Add the cream cheese, double cream, honey and 1 tbsp of the chopped thyme and mix together briskly until it forms soft, billowy peaks.

Once cooked, take the cakes out of the oven and leave to cool in the tins for 10 minutes before turning out onto a wire rack to cool completely. Once cool, spread a third of the frosting on the top of one cake, pop the other cake on top and cover the whole thing liberally and messily with the rest of the frosting. Sprinkle with the remaining thyme leaves and flowers (if you have some) and serve. The cake will keep in an airtight container in a cool place (but not a fridge) for a couple of days.

Ken Hom
Thai-inspired mixed vegetable salad

I have always loved the idea of warm salads, especially with vegetables. Inspired by Thai flavours, this makes a great, vegetarian starter or can be served with other dishes as part of a main course.

Vegan
Serves 4

For the Thai dressing

2 small red Thai chillies, seeded and chopped

2 tbsp light soy sauce

2 tsp sugar

1 tsp freshly ground 5 pepper or black pepper

4 tbsp lime juice

For the salad

225g tomatoes

100g small broccoli florets

100g green beans (haricot verts), trimmed

100g small cauliflower florets

100g fresh or frozen peas

3 tbsp shallots, finely chopped, squeezed dry with a cloth

3 tbsp fresh basil, finely chopped

Make the Thai dressing by combining the chillies, soy sauce, sugar, pepper and lime juice. Mix well and set aside.

Bring a pot of salted water to the boil. Drop in the tomatoes for 5 seconds, remove, peel and seed. Cut the tomatoes into 4cm pieces and set aside.

Now add the broccoli, green beans and cauliflower and cook for 3 minutes, then add the peas and cook for 1 minute.

Drain the vegetables into a warm bowl, then add in the chopped tomato. Drizzle over the Thai dressing and add the shallots and basil. Mix well and serve at once.

Özlem Warren
Baked cauliflower with red onions, feta and dill: *firinda karnabahar mucveri*

During one of my culinary tours to Turkey, we had a Turkish cooking class at the Bizimev Hanimeli Restaurant, near the charming Sirince in the Aegean region. We made lightly battered, delicious cauliflower fritters as part of our class. Inspired by this dish, I created this version and tried baking cauliflower with beyaz peynir or feta, dill and onions in the oven. The result was a great success – baking brought out a sweetness in the cauliflower which balanced nicely with the sharp feta; a lovely dish, packed with flavour. Diced red pepper also works well in this dish.

I serve this baked cauliflower with cacik yoghurt dip with cucumbers and shepherd's salad with sumac onions. It can be served hot or at room temperature with a grilled main course and lemon wedges on the side.

Serves 6

1 medium cauliflower, cut into very small florets

1 small red onion, finely chopped

2 garlic cloves, finely chopped

3 spring onions, finely chopped

small bunch of flat leaf parsley, finely chopped

small bunch of fresh dill, finely chopped

2 tbsp olive oil

200g feta or Turkish white cheese, beyaz peynir, drained and crumbled

2 tsp Turkish red pepper flakes, pul biber or chili flakes (use less if preferred)

salt and freshly ground black pepper to taste

3 medium eggs, beaten

4 tbsp all-purpose/plain flour

22cm x 22cm baking dish to bake

1 tbsp olive oil to grease the baking dish

wedges of lemon to serve

Preheat the oven to 180°C/160°C fan.

Cut the cauliflower into very small florets, wash and drain the excess water in a colander.

Place the cauliflower florets in a large mixing bowl. Stir in the chopped red onions, garlic, spring onions, parsley, dill, olive oil and the crumbled feta cheese to the bowl. Season with salt, ground black pepper and Turkish red pepper flakes or chili flakes.

With clean hands, mix and combine all the ingredients well. At this stage, you can check the seasoning – add more salt or pepper to your taste. Then stir in the beaten eggs and flour to the cauliflower mixture and combine well.

Grease your baking dish with 1 tbsp olive oil and spread the mixture to the baking dish. Bake in the preheated oven for 30–35 minutes, until the cauliflower florets have a nice, light brown colour on top.

Slice and serve hot or at room temperature with a wedge of lemon at the side.

Afiyet olsun.

The Kew kitchen garden

Thomasina Miers
Bean and charred corn tostada with jalapeno aioli

Ching-He Huang
Ching's Buddha's Veggie Chow Mein

Selina Periampillai
Creole saffran rice

Niki Segnit
Ful medames

Sefanit Sophie Sirak-Kebede
Ethiopian teff *enjera*: traditional fermented flat bread

Luiz Hara
Brown butter and miso linguine

Sumayya Usmani
Karachi spiced lentil and potato bun kebabs

Sami Tamimi
Aubergine, chickpea and tomato bake: *musaqa'a*

GRAINS AND PULSES

Irina Georgescu
Barley crêpes with honey hemp cream: *clătite din orz cu julfă*

Jenny Chandler
Roasted beetroot, plum and carlin pea salad

Kimiko Barber
Asparagus and scrambled egg scattered sushi bowl

Chetna Makan
Red kidney beans and potato curry: *Rajma alu* curry

Tom Hunt
Emmer wheat salad with apricots, broad beans and seaweed

Rachel Roddy
Braised lentils with pan-fried porcini

Zaleha Kadir Olpin
Sticky rice bon bon: *pulut sambal*

Dan Lepard
Marmalade wholegrain tart

The edible seeds we call grains and pulses are truly fundamental foods. They play a special part in human history. The planting of seed-bearing grains and legumes around 11,000 years ago was the beginning of human agriculture. In the Middle East, in an area known as 'the Fertile Crescent', eight plants are thought to be the founder crops in this region: three cereals, four pulses and flax. In Asia, at around the same time, rice and millet began to be cultivated, while in Mexico, maize, descended from a grass called teosinte, began to be planted. The ability to provide a source of food by growing crops saw early humans shift from hunting and gathering to a more settled existence, underpinned by a pattern of planting and harvesting.

Remarkably, just three grains – rice, maize and wheat – continue to provide 60 per cent of the world's food energy intake. We do also eat other grains, among them, barley, rye, millet, oats, quinoa, sorghum and teff. Over the centuries, humans have been remarkably ingenious at transforming dry, hard grains into a variety of foods. The most basic way of eating grains is to soften them by cooking them whole in liquid. Another response to the hardness of grains was to break them down by grinding them. Flour made from grains such as maize, wheat or teff is used to make bread – a historic staple – in many forms. There are flatbreads – the Mexican tortillas, Indian chapati and paratha, Ethiopian *enjera* – and also leavened breads, made using raising agents such as a sourdough starter or yeast, including the French baguette, Russian rye bread or Italian ciabatta. Flour is also the starting point from which we make noodles and pasta, with the Chinese the first to transform grain into both noodles and filled pasta shapes. Within European cuisine, Italy is noted for its rich diversity of pasta shapes and recipes. The speed with which pasta shapes such as spaghetti or egg noodles can be plunged into boiling water and transformed into a family meal is much appreciated by busy cooks around the world. Flour, of course, is also used to make cakes, pastries, biscuits, fritters and pancakes – the historic treats one finds in cuisines throughout the globe. Grains don't just feed human beings directly, they are also used to feed livestock such as cattle, pigs and chicken. Furthermore, it is not just food that we use grains for but alcoholic drinks, such as beer and spirits.

The edible seeds of the legume (Fabaceae) family – the plant family which has the highest number of known edible species (625) – have nourished humans around the globe for thousands of years. Pulses (one group of edible legumes) have long been an important source of protein, especially in vegetarian diets, and are also low in fat and cholesterol free. Drying is an effective way of preserving them without adversely affecting their flavour, making them a useful addition to the store cupboard. Furthermore, many pulses enrich the soil by fixing nitrogen, through an association with bacteria in their root nodules, leaving it as a natural fertiliser for other crops, with legumes used in crop rotation in different countries for centuries.

A wide variety of pulses are consumed around the world. Iconic dishes include America's Boston baked beans, Brazil's feijoada, Egypt's *ful medames*, France's socca, Israel's falafel, Italy's pasta fagioli and Jamaica's rice and peas. Indian cuisine is noted for its extensive use of pulses in a variety of dishes including pancakes made from fermented lentils, purées, fritters, soups and curries. The soya bean plays a central role in Chinese and Japanese cuisines. Dried soya beans are transformed into both soya bean milk and bean curd, which is eaten in fresh, dried and fermented forms. Soya beans are also ground into a paste and fermented to make soy sauce, that umami-rich condiment essential in Chinese and Japanese cooking. Miso paste made from fermented soya beans is a key ingredient in Japanese cuisine, used to flavour soups, spread on grilled foods or as the base for dressings. When it comes to using whole dried pulses, such as butter beans or cannellini beans, soaking them beforehand in cold water overnight reduces their cooking time considerably and helps them cook through evenly and well. Split and de-hulled pulses such as split lentils do not require pre-soaking before cooking.

Given the importance of grains and pulses in feeding our ever-growing human population, much work is being done at Kew to safeguard these essential foods. Part of this work focuses on banking the seeds of crop wild relatives and conserving genetic variation in crops as well as finding forms resilient to future changes in climate and other environmental factors. Although there are almost 12,000 species in the Poaceae (grass) family, few have been widely introduced into cultivation in the last 200 years. Rice, which feeds almost half of humanity, is under threat from a changing climate: extreme temperatures can stress the plants or stop them growing at all, flooding can destroy paddy fields where rice is grown and increased humidity can lead to the spread of diseases. Kew scientists have been working alongside the Crop Trust, collecting seeds from the wild relatives of rice and storing them in Kew's Millennium Seed Bank, as a conserved resource for future generations. Kew is also collaborating with the International Rice Research Institute in the Philippines and sending them wild rice species for research purposes.

Scientists at Kew highlighted the need for more diverse, resilient and sustainable food production systems in their 2020 *State of the World's Plants and Fungi* report. Part of their work is to identify potential future crops. Among these, they highlight fonio, a fast-growing grass species that grows wild across the savannas of West Africa and which is cultivated locally as a cereal crop. High in iron, calcium and essential amino acids, fonio (*Digitaria exilis*) can tolerate and survive dry conditions. Another possible, more widely cultivated future food is the morama bean (*Tylosema esculentum*), a drought-tolerant trailing plant native to arid parts of southern Africa. The beans are eaten widely, roasted, boiled with maize meal or ground to a powder to make porridge or a hot drink. The beans also yield oil, butter and milk and are a source of good quality protein.

Kew's vast and comprehensive Herbarium collection, with its goldmine of rich historical records, has a pivotal role to play in adding to knowledge about legumes, including overlooked crops such as the hyacinth bean (*Lablab purpureus*) or edible lupin (*Lupinus mutabilis*). Mass digitisation is putting more of Kew's information online, allowing researchers digital access to taxonomic, ecological and geographical data. Over 37,000 legume specimens of a total c.750,000 at Kew have now been digitised. This online data can be used to extract information about species traits valuable to plant breeders and which may mitigate future climate change.

There is still much to learn about a plant family that has already given us peas, beans, chickpeas, lentils, soya beans, peanuts and many more food crops. Peanuts, originating in the Americas, today are a multibillion-dollar crop grown across Asia, Africa, Australia and North and South America, yet the cultivated crop (*Arachis hypogaea*) is only one of 69 peanut species found in the wild. There is a lot to discover about the biology of the other 68 species. Deepening our knowledge and understanding of food crops and their many wild relatives is crucial to sustainable agriculture and the survival of humankind.

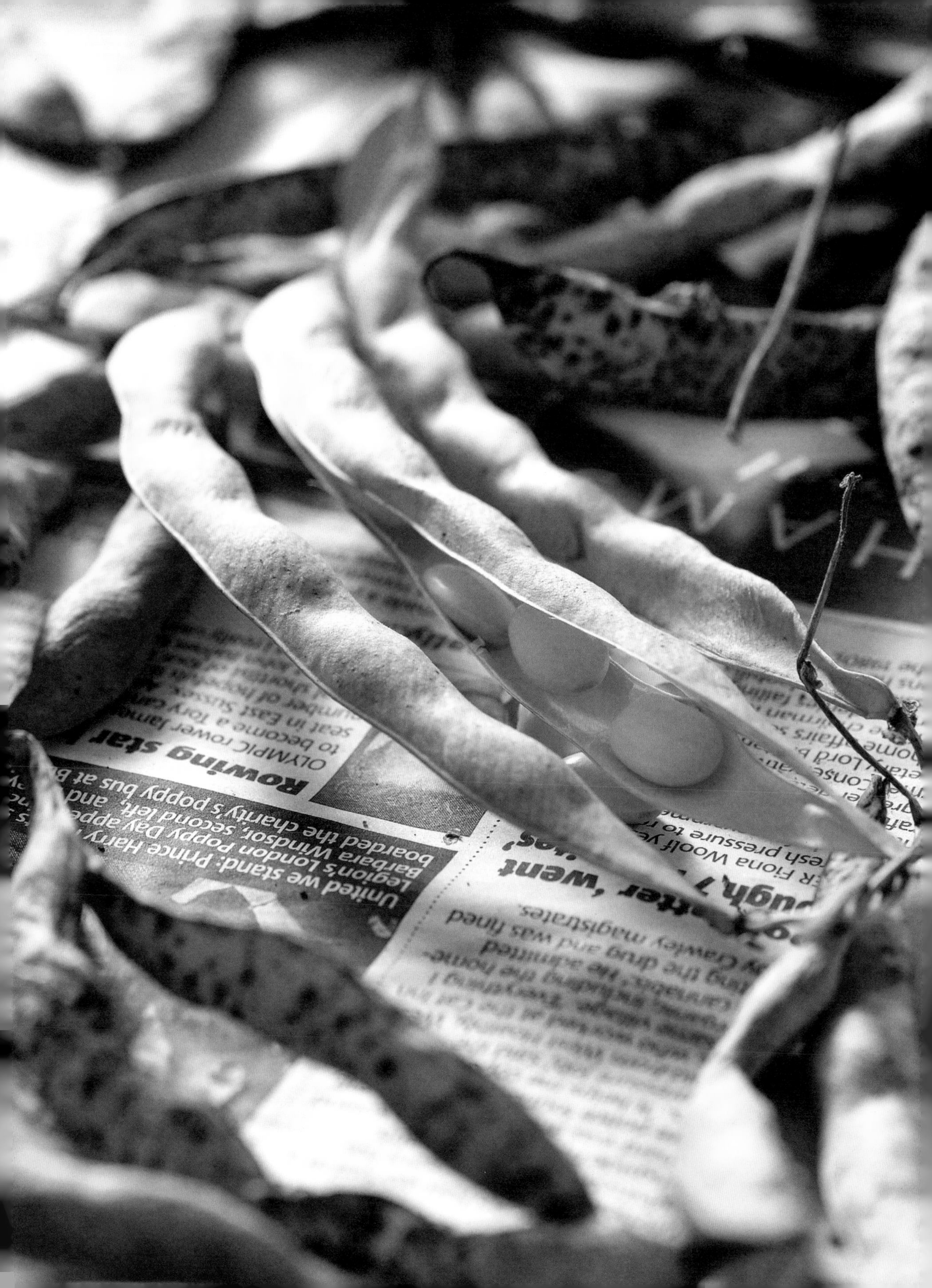
Rowing star
OLYMPIC rower
United we stand: Prince Harry

The Great Broad Walk Borders

Thomasina Miers

Bean and charred corn tostada with jalapeno aioli

We have had versions of this vibrant, rich-tasting bean salad on the menus at Wahaca since we opened. In the late summer I like to toss in charred corn which is delicious on a crispy corn tortilla, especially when spread with a garlicky roast jalapeno aioli. The dangerously delicious aioli adds a silky background note to the whole, an extra lick of flavour, a blend of fresh lime, sparkly chilli heat, umami garlic, moving an otherwise wholesome dish to something infinitely more compelling, both naughty and nice. Late summer corn and the ripest summer tomatoes with a grilled garlicky chilli mayo on a crispy tortilla base. These are my kind of flavours...if you prefer you can use the water from your tins of beans/chickpeas to bind the mayo instead of eggs.

Feeds 4

4 corn on the cobs

vegetable oil, for grilling/frying

2 x tins Hodmedod's beans and/or chickpeas, drained

1 tbsp apple cider vinegar

2 tbsp good olive oil

12 limes, juice and zest

250g cherry tomatoes, halved

red onion, finely sliced

a large bunch of coriander, about 60g, washed

2–3 jalapenos or other fresh green chillies

8–12 small corn tortillas, or 6 pittas

To garnish

1–2 tbsp feta, optional

1–2 radishes, finely sliced

For the aioli

2 egg yolks

1 fat clove garlic

juice of a lime

100ml vegetable oil

100ml extra virgin olive oil

First char the corn, using a griddle pan or a bbq. Remove the husks from the corn, rub the cobs in a little vegetable oil and sprinkle with sea salt. Griddle/grill for 6–8 minutes or until blackened, turning often.

Let the corn cool and then use a sharp knife to remove the kernels. Toss with the beans, vinegar, 2 tbsp olive oil, lime juice, tomatoes and onion. Add a few tbsp finely chopped coriander stalks and one of the chillies, sliced wafer thin. Taste and adjust the seasoning. Meanwhile heat an inch of oil in a deep frying pan and when sizzling hot fry the tortillas until crisp. If you are using pittas, cut out circles to the size of tostada you want using a cookie cutter and fry until crisp too (or brush with oil and bake until crisp if you prefer). Drain the tostadas on kitchen towel.

To make the aioli toast the remaining chillies in a small dry frying pan over a high heat for 7–8 minutes until blackened all over. De-stalk and add one to a food blender with the egg yolks, garlic, rest of the coriander, roughly chopped, ½ tsp of sea salt and the lime juice. Blitz to a paste and then slowly, slowly pour in 100ml vegetable oil in a thin, steady stream. Continue to pour the oil in as the aioli emulsifies, until it is all incorporated. Now add 100ml of olive oil in a faster stream and once incorporated taste and adjust the seasoning by adding a little more chilli, lime juice, salt or a pinch of caster sugar.

Spread the aioli on the bottom of the tostadas, top with the bean salad and add a few slices of radish and a crumble of feta, if you would like. Serve as a starter, light lunch or part of a spread.

Ching-He Huang
Ching's Buddha's Veggie Chow Mein

This is the kind of dish that allows you to use up any leftover vegetables and is so easy using store cupboard ingredients. I love adding some slices of smoked tofu for texture and protein. Of course, use whichever noodles you like but I love organic soybean noodles which are high in protein, are gluten free and high in fibre too. They have a slight beany flavour too. This dish is not only packed with more than your five-a-day veggies, it's aromatic and delicious. It's perfect as a mid-week supper or a feasting dish for family and friends.

Vegan
Serves 4 to share

200g (dried weight) organic soybean noodles

1 tsp toasted sesame oil

1 tbsp rapeseed oil

2 cloves of garlic, peeled and finely chopped

2.5cm of freshly grated root ginger

2 large red chilli, deseeded, sliced into julienne strips

1 large carrot, topped, tailed, sliced into julienne strips

10 fresh shiitake mushrooms sliced

1 small handful of mangetout, washed, sliced into julienne

200g baby corn, sliced in half on the angle down the middle

2 baby pak choy, washed, halved down the middle

1 tbsp Shaoxing rice wine or dry sherry

200g smoked tofu with sesame seeds, (optional), sliced to julienne

▶▶

Combine all the ingredients for the sauce, mix well and place in a jug.

Cook the organic soybean noodles in boiling water for 3 minutes. Drain and refresh the noodles in cold water. Dress with 1 tsp toasted sesame oil, mix well and set aside.

Prepare all the rest of the ingredients.

Heat a wok over high heat and add the rapeseed oil. Add the garlic, ginger, chilli and stir-fry for a few seconds, add the carrot and stir-fry for 1 minute, add the shiitake, mangetout, baby corn and pak choy leaves and toss, cooking for a few seconds. Add in the rice wine. Stir gently for 1 minute. Add the smoked tofu slices.

Pour in the sauce and bring to the bubble, cooking for less than a minute until the sauce is shiny. Toss the noodles and gently fold them in, mixing the noodles with the ingredients and sauce together in the wok, but being careful not to 'stab' at the noodles or ingredients. Season with 1 tbsp tamari.

Finally sprinkle in the beansprouts and give it one last stir together.

Spoon out and sprinkle over spring onion curls, toasted cashew nuts and black sesame seeds. Place on the table and serve with other dishes or spoon into individual serving plates. Serve with Chiu Chow chilli oil on the side.

▶▶

1 tbsp tamari

100g beansprouts

2 large spring onions, julienne, placed in cold iced water to give 'curls'

1 large handful of toasted cashew nuts

1 tbsp black sesame seeds

For the sauce

100ml cold vegetable stock

1 tbsp tamari or low sodium light soy sauce

1 tbsp vegetarian mushroom sauce

1 tbsp toasted sesame oil

1 tbsp rice vinegar

1 tbsp cornflour

Chiu Chow chilli oil, to serve

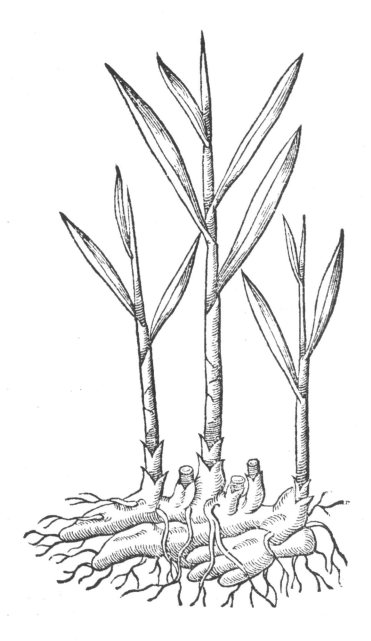

Selina Periampillai
Creole saffran rice

For me, rice is an empty canvas waiting to be experimented with. When I had this dish in a local guesthouse in Mahé in the Seychelles, I marvelled at its vibrant colours: it was bright with sweet, crunchy peppers and fresh herbs, and gorgeously aromatic with spices. 'Saffran' is the Creole term for the spice turmeric, which is freshly grated into the rice or ground and then added to give it a beautiful colour.

Basmati rice, with its slender grains, is perfect for this dish; however, you can use jasmine as an alternative. Always soak or wash the rice grains first in cold water until the water runs clear. This will get rid of any impurities and make the rice much fluffier when cooked.

Vegan
Serves 4

200g basmati rice

2 tbsp olive oil

1 large shallot or small onion, finely chopped

2 garlic cloves, finely chopped

2.5cm piece of fresh root ginger, peeled and finely chopped

5 curry leaves, fresh or dried

1 red pepper, diced

1 tsp ground turmeric

½ tsp ground cinnamon

2 tbsp chopped parsley

sea salt and freshly ground black pepper

Firstly soak the rice for 30 minutes in cold water (or wash a few times until the water runs clear). Drain well. Cook your rice in accordance with the packet instructions.

Meanwhile, heat the olive oil in a medium saucepan over a medium heat. Fry the shallot or onion with the garlic, ginger and curry leaves for 5–7 minutes, stirring occasionally.

Add in the diced red pepper and ½ tsp sea salt and cook for 2–3 minutes, until slightly softened but still retaining its crunch. Sprinkle over the turmeric and cinnamon and mix well into the ingredients.

When the rice is cooked, stir it into the shallot mixture until it is yellow all over. Sprinkle over salt and pepper to season and scatter over the parsley leaves. Give it one more gentle mix and spoon onto a platter to serve.

Niki Segnit
Ful medames

Fava beans were once an important crop in Britain, and the Suffolk-based bean and pulse company Hodmedod's have made it their mission to bring them back. *Ful medames* is probably the world's most popular application for beans like these, perhaps because of the garnishes, which can take the richly flavoured beans in any direction your appetite fancies – sulphurous, mineral, sharp, bitter or earthy.

Serves 4

300g fava beans with their skins on, soaked in cold water for about 8 hours

4 eggs

4–6 tomatoes

1–2 lemons

a handful of flat leaf parsley leaves

1 tbsp cumin seeds

1 garlic clove, chopped fine

olive oil

optional: tahini

warm pita breads, to serve

Drain and rinse the soaked beans. Put them in a pan with enough fresh water to cover them, plus an extra centimetre or two. Bring to the boil, then put the lid on the pan. Turn down the heat until the water is at a simmer, then cook for at least 30 minutes before checking if the beans are soft. If they're not, they might need anything up to 30 minutes longer. Check every 10 minutes. Add a little salt when they seem almost cooked.

While the beans are cooking, prepare your garnishes. Boil the eggs to your preferred softness. I like the velvety yolk you get after about 7 minutes (if the eggs started out at room temperature). Remove the eggs from the water and set aside to cool.

Cut the tomatoes and lemons into wedges. Chop the parsley.

Toast 1 tbsp cumin seeds over a low-medium heat for as long as they take to colour a bit and turn fragrant. Keep an eagle eye on them: they can burn in the blink of an eye. Cool, then grind.

Peel and halve the eggs lengthways.

Place the halved eggs, tomatoes, lemons, parsley, ground cumin and tahini in separate dishes.

Drain the hot beans, then stir in the chopped garlic and olive oil to taste.

Divide the beans into bowls and invite your guests to customise them with the garnishes.

Sefanit Sophie Sirak-Kebede

Ethiopian teff *enjera*: traditional fermented flat bread

Teff, the tiny seed considered a grain, is remarkable in many ways. Cultivated in Ethiopia for thousands of years, it is very hardy, growing well in both dry and waterlogged soils. Once sown, a single pound of teff can yield a tonne of grain in around 12 weeks. It is gluten-free and high in calcium and magnesium.

Teff occupies a special place in Ethiopian cuisine. *Enjera*, the tangy, fermented flatbread central to meals in Ethiopia, is made from teff flour. Bear in mind, that 7 days of fermenting are required for this recipe in order to achieve the distinctive sour tang which is so characteristic of *enjera*.

Vegan

**Makes 7–8 *enjera*
(each around 40cm across),
depending on their thickness**

For the starter
250g teff flour
300ml lukewarm water

For the teff *enjera*
1kg teff flour
1.2l water

First, make the starter. Mix the teff flour with the lukewarm water until thoroughly mixed. Cover and set aside in the refridgerator for 3 days to ferment.

To make the *enjera*, whisk together the flour and 600ml water in a large bowl until it has the consistency of pancake batter. Add in the starter, mixing in well. Cover and set aside for 3 days in a warm place to ferment. Bear in mind, that the fermentation process may vary depending on the weather.

On the fourth day, bring 600ml of water to the boil in a large pan. Mix in 300ml of the fermented *enjera* batter. Simmer for 6–7 minutes over a low heat, stirring constantly.

Pour this hot mixture back into the original *enjera* batter and stir well to combine. Cover and leave it overnight in a warm place.

To make the teff *enjera*, you need either an Ethiopian metad (an eathernware flat skillet) or a large, flat-bottomed, non-stick frying pan or a paella pan. Heat the pan over a medium heat. Pour in a little of the batter, spreading it around the pan evenly to the thickness of a thin pancake. Cover and cook for approximately 60–90 seconds. As it cooks, lots of bubbles (like the ones you find on crumpets) should form on the surface.

Remove the *enjera* from the pan and set aside to cool. Repeat the process until all the mixture has been used. Bear in mind that the cooled teff *enjera* can be rolled up and frozen.

Luiz Hara
Brown butter and miso linguine

This is a super easy, quick mid-week dinner and a fantastic way to introduce Japanese miso into your everyday cooking. It is also terribly addictive. Different miso brands will vary in saltiness, so always check and adjust the quantities if necessary.

**Serves 4 as a starter
or 2 as a main**

For the pasta
200g dried linguine pasta
2 tbsp pine nuts
2 tbsp chopped flat leaf parsley
freshly ground black pepper
2 tbsp Parmesan cheese,
freshly grated
micro parsley or basil (optional)

For the sauce
75g unsalted butter
1 banana shallot, peeled and
finely sliced
2 tbsp light brown or white
miso paste

In a large pan filled with boiling salted water, cook the linguine until al dente following the packet instructions. Drain, reserving some of the cooking liquor.

Meanwhile, dry-fry the pine nuts in a non-stick frying pan until lightly golden, then roughly chop and set aside until needed.

Make the sauce in the same frying pan. Melt the butter, stirring from time to time. When the butter starts to brown and smell slightly nutty, lower the heat and add the shallot, coating it in the butter. Cook for a couple of minutes until the shallot is softened, remove from the heat, then add the brown miso paste and a few tablespoons of the reserved pasta cooking liquor. Using a whisk, mix the miso vigorously into the browned butter until the sauce is well combined, creamy and lump-free.

Add the drained pasta to the pan with the sauce and add the pine nuts, parsley and black pepper and toss well. Finish off with a generous sprinkle of Parmesan cheese and some micro parsley or basil, if you wish, and serve immediately.

Sumayya Usmani
Karachi spiced lentil and potato bun kebabs

I'd crave these vegetarian kebabs-in-a-bun on hot afternoons – they define the explosive flavour of Karachi street snacks, bringing together spiced tamarind and green chutney toppings. We'd buy the traditional version of this burger from the street sides. It came hot in a greasy brown paper bag, begging to be devoured and then washed down with Pakola – a ubiquitous, green, saccharin-sweet fizzy soft drink.

Serves 4–6

For the kebabs

60g chana daal

3 Maris Piper potatoes

3 egg whites, beaten to soft peaks

4 tbsp ghee

6–8 tbsp vegetable oil

4–6 burger buns

6 tsp tamarind chutney or sauce (buy ready-made)

6 tsp green chutney (see recipe overleaf)

6 tbsp tomato ketchup or chilli garlic sauce

1–2 tomatoes, cut into round slices

½ cucumber, cut into thin, round slices

For the spices

2 tsp ground cumin

1 tsp ground coriander seeds

2 tsp chaat masala

1 tsp red chilli powder

1 tsp sea salt, or to taste

►►

Soak the chana daal in a bowl of water for 2 hours, then drain and boil in enough water to cover them for 30 minutes, or until soft. Drain and set aside. Meanwhile, peel the potatoes and boil in a large saucepan until soft.

To make the kebabs, mash the potatoes, spices, salt and cooked daal together in a large bowl using a fork. Using a tablespoon, scoop out 2 tbsp of the spiced mash and form into 10cm round burger-style patties.

Put the beaten egg white into a shallow bowl. Heat 1 tbsp each of ghee and oil (this should be enough to cook 1 patty) in a non-stick frying pan over a medium-low heat. Dip each patty into the beaten egg white and fry for about 2–3 minutes on each side until light brown.

Place each cooked patty on a plate and cover with another plate to keep warm. Once all the patties are cooked and ready to serve, cut the burger buns in half. Heat about ½ tsp each of the ghee and vegetable oil in a flat griddle pan or frying pan and fry all 4 sides of each bun until caramelised and crispy, about 2 minutes on each side.

Repeat until all the buns are fried. Place a patty on the bottom fried bun, top with tamarind sauce, green chutney, tomato ketchup or chilli garlic sauce, and a slice of tomato and cucumber, if you like, then cover with the top side of the bun. Serve with more of the sauces.

►►

**For the green chutney
(makes about 150–200ml)**

1 large bunch of
coriander leaves

10–12 mint leaves

1 small green chilli,
deseeded

½ tbsp brown sugar
or jaggery

½ tsp ground turmeric

1 tsp dry-roasted
cumin seeds

1 tsp salt

2 tbsp unsweetened
desiccated (dry) coconut

Juice of ½ lime

4 tbsp water

Make the green chutney as follows:

This is a classic green chutney, aromatic, and exotic, and with many uses. You can make it as dip, side sauce or marinade – if you want a lighter, less spiced option, just mix with 2–3 tbsp plain yoghurt.

Blitz all the ingredients in a blender until it is smooth. This is best used immediately but can be stored in an airtight container in the fridge for up to 4–5 days.

Sami Tamimi

Aubergine, chickpea and tomato bake: *musaqa'a*

Echoes of the Greek dish moussaka are correctly heard here, both in the name and the feel of the dish. It's a vegetarian take on the hearty, humble, healthy and completely delicious traybake. It works well either as a veggie main or as a side with all sorts of things: piled into a jacket potato, for example, or served alongside some grilled meat, fish or tofu. It's just the sort of dish you want to have in the fridge ready to greet you after a day out at work. It's also lovely at room temperature, so it's great to pile into the Tupperware for an on-the-go lunch.

Vegan

Serves 4 as a main or 6 as a side

5 medium aubergines (1.25kg)

120ml olive oil

1 onion, finely chopped (160g)

6 garlic cloves, crushed

1 tsp chilli flakes

1 tsp ground cumin

½ tsp ground cinnamon

1½ tsp tomato purée

2 green peppers, deseeded and cut into 3cm chunks (200g)

1 x 400g tin of chickpeas, drained and rinsed (240g)

1 x 400g tin of chopped tomatoes

1½ tsp caster sugar

15g coriander, roughly chopped, plus 5g extra to serve

4 plum tomatoes, trimmed and sliced into 1½cm thick rounds (350g)

salt and black pepper

Preheat the oven to 240°C/220°C fan.

Use a vegetable peeler to peel away strips of aubergine skin from top to bottom, leaving the aubergines with alternating strips of black skin and white flesh, like a zebra. Cut widthways into round slices, 2cm thick, and place in a large bowl. Mix well with 75ml of oil, 1 tsp salt and plenty of black pepper and spread out on two large parchment-lined baking trays. Roast for about 30 minutes, or until completely softened and lightly browned. Remove from the oven and set aside.

Reduce the oven temperature to 200°C/180°C fan.

While the aubergines are roasting, make the sauce. Put 2 tbsp oil into a large sauté pan and place on a medium-high heat. Add the onion and cook for about 7 minutes, until softened and lightly browned. Add the garlic, chilli, cumin, cinnamon and tomato purée and cook for another minute, or until fragrant. Add the peppers, chickpeas, tinned tomatoes, sugar, 200ml of water, 1¼ tsp salt and a good grind of black pepper. Reduce the heat to medium and cook for 18 minutes, or until the peppers have cooked through. Stir in the coriander and remove from the heat.

Spread out half the plum tomatoes and half the roasted aubergines on the base of a large baking dish, about 20cm x 30cm. Top with the chickpea mixture, then layer with the remaining tomatoes and aubergines. Drizzle with the remaining tablespoon of oil, then cover with foil and bake for 30 minutes. Remove the foil and bake for another 20 minutes, or until the sauce is bubbling and the tomatoes have completely softened. Remove from the oven and leave to cool for about 20 minutes. Top with the remaining coriander and serve either warm or at room temperature.

Getting ahead

You can make and bake this in advance: it keeps in the fridge for up to 3 days, ready to be warmed through when needed.

Irina Georgescu
Barley crêpes with honey hemp cream: *clătite din orz cu julfă*

This hemp cream, made with honey and topped with walnuts, is a speciality from Moldova, Romania, called *julfă*. With hemp being a traditional crop (though unfortunately largely forgotten today), the cream has only remained in culinary use to make a sort of layered pie at Christmas. The thin pancakes draw inspiration from this pie and are easier to make, while the barley flour gives them a delicious, rich and nutty flavour.

Serves 6

For the barley crêpes
150g barley flour
320ml oat milk
(or any non-dairy milk)
2 large eggs
20ml honey
sunflower oil for frying

For the hemp cream
250g shelled hemp seeds (also called hemp hearts)
35ml honey
125ml oat milk (or any non-dairy milk or water)

To serve
honey for drizzling
30g chopped walnuts

Make the crêpes by putting the flour in a bowl. In a measuring mug, mix together the oat milk, eggs and honey. Make a well in the middle of the flour and pour the liquid in gradually, stirring constantly to avoid the forming of lumps. Place in the fridge for 1 hour.

Lightly oil a non-stick, 22cm diameter frying pan and heat through. Pour a ladle of the batter in the middle, and tilt the pan around at once so that the batter spreads evenly. Cook for 2 minutes on medium heat, then flip the pancake over and cook for a further 2 minutes. Set aside on a plate and repeat the process with the remaining batter.

Make the hemp cream by placing the hemp seeds and honey into a food processor. Pulse together 3 times, then with the motor running on medium speed, start adding the milk. It should have a smooth, spreadable consistency, but you can add more milk if you prefer it thinner.

Fill each crêpe with a generous tablespoon of hemp cream, fold into four or roll like a cigar, drizzle with honey and sprinkle the walnuts on top. *Poftă bună*, bon appetit.

Note
The cream goes wonderfully well with roasted fruit or jam. You can also replace half the quantity of hemp hearts with pumpkin seeds, for a slightly different flavour. Make it savoury by omitting the honey and adding a clove of garlic and fresh herbs.

Jenny Chandler
Roasted beetroot, plum and carlin pea salad

A sweet and sour, late summer salad with the carlin peas creating a satisfyingly filling backdrop for the seasonal fruit and veg. Carlin peas have been part of the foodscape in the North and Midlands for centuries, but have recently become more widely available, thanks to a pioneering company called Hodmedods who sell a huge range of sustainable British pulses, grains and seeds. You could use chickpeas or lentils in their place, but the nutty flavour of the carlin pea is so worth seeking out.

Serves 4 as a main

600g raw beetroot (about 6 medium beets)

3 tbsp olive oil

good pinch of salt

2 small red onions

8 ripe plums

1 tsp cumin seeds

1 tsp chilli flakes

2 garlic cloves, finely chopped

100g walnut pieces

3 tbsp extra virgin olive oil

2–3 tbsp cider vinegar

salt, pepper and perhaps a dash of honey or brown sugar to taste

600g cooked carlin peas, drained (home-cooked (see note at end of recipe) or 2 x 400g can, drained)

a large handful of dill, mint or parsley, roughly chopped

Preheat the oven to 190°C/170°C fan.

Wash the beetroot well, and cut in half if the beets are particularly large. Place them onto a large sheet of foil in a roasting tin, drizzle over half of the olive oil and season with the salt. Now fold over the foil, making a loose tent. Roast for 45 minutes to an hour until they are tender (and then the skins will slip off easily).

Meanwhile, peel and chop each of the onions through the root into about 10 thin segments. Halve and stone the plums. Place the onions and plums in roasting tin, drizzle over the remaining oil and season with a little salt, the cumin seeds and chilli flakes. Roast these in the same oven for about 15 minutes before sprinkling over the garlic and walnuts and cooking for 10 more minutes, then set aside to cool.

Make the dressing by mixing together the extra virgin olive oil, cider vinegar, salt and pepper (adding a little honey, or sugar, if your plums were quite tart). Stir the carlin peas around in half of the dressing and add half of the herbs.

Slip the skins off the beetroot and cut into bite-sized, irregular chunks.

Now arrange the salad on a large platter – carlin peas first, scattered with the beets, plums, onion, walnuts, remaining dressing and herbs.

You could:

• Use a mixture of golden and classic red beetroot

• Crumble over 150g feta cheese or serve with seasoned Greek yoghurt

• Replace the roasted plums with segments of raw blood orange in late winter

Cooking carlin peas (or any whole, dried peas for that matter)
Soak the peas overnight (you can add a teaspoon of bicarbonate of soda to speed up the cooking if you live somewhere with hard water). Drain the peas, place in a large pan and cover with plenty of cold water. Cover and simmer for about 45 minutes to an hour, until the peas are soft and creamy within, but still hold their shape. Season with salt.

The Millennium Seed
Bank, Wakehurst

Kimiko Barber
Asparagus and scrambled egg scattered sushi bowl

Sushi is arguably the best known and best loved dish in Japanese cuisine. It is made of two essential components – *neta,* materials and *shari,* vinegar flavoured rice. Although a fatty slice of tuna is often the choice material, vegetables and eggs make a good *neta.* Sushi masters and connoisseurs pay attention to *shari,* because well cooked and seasoned rice makes the perfect foundation to bring out the taste of any materials.

Sushi doesn't have to be a roll or bite-size nugget, but also comes in many different styles; some are easier and need no specialist equipment or techniques. Scattered sushi is a free-style, simple rice salad which can be made with any vegetables of your choice. If you wish to make easy and tasty, vegetarian sushi, this recipe is for you.

Serves 4

For sushi rice
300g Japanese-style short grain rice
330ml soft mineral water or once-boiled and cooled tap water
1 postcard-size piece of dried kombu/kelp (optional)
4 tbsp Japanese rice vinegar
2 tbsp sugar
½ tsp sea salt

For toppings
2 eggs
1 egg yolk
½ tsp salt
1 tsp sugar
1 tsp vegetable oil
400g asparagus
100g sugar snap peas
6 baby vine tomatoes, cut in half

1 tbsp toasted sesame seeds for garnish

Good sushi always begins with well cooked rice. Sushi rice is cooked with slightly less water than if you are cooking plain boiled rice to allow some room for the addition of sushi vinegar. Put the rice in a sieve submerged in a large bowl filled with cold water. Use your hand to wash and discard the milky water – keep rinsing and changing water until it becomes clear; this usually takes 3–5 times water changes.

Drain and put the rice and measured water with the kombu (if using, make a few slashes to help release more umami flavour) in a heavy-based saucepan with a tight-fitting lid and let it stand for 15 minutes before turning on the heat. This soaking period is particularly important to let the rice absolve moisture and cook evenly. Over medium heat, bring to the boil, then increase the heat slightly and cook for a further 3–5 minutes. Reduce the heat to low and simmer for a further 10 minutes, then turn off the heat and let it steam for another 10–15 minutes before lifting the lid and discarding the kombu.

While the rice is cooking, mix together the rice vinegar, sugar and salt to make sushi vinegar. Prepare the toppings. For the scrambled egg, mix together the eggs and yolk with the salt and sugar. Lightly oil a non-stick pan over medium heat and pour in the egg mixture and cook stirring constantly with two pairs of chopsticks or a whisk. When the eggs begin to set, remove the pan from the heat but continue stirring to get a fluffy consistency. Set aside to cool down.

▶▶

Discard the woody base part of each asparagus stalk and cut into fingertip size pieces. Cut the sugar snap peas into the similar size pieces. Blanch both vegetables in a pan of boiling water for 2–3 minutes, then immediately plunge them into a bowl of ice-cold water and dry thoroughly to keep their vibrant green colour.

Moisten a *hangiri* (Japanese shallow wooden tub that is specially designed for preparing sushi rice). If you don't have one, use a wide glass, ceramic or plastic mixing bowl instead. Place the cooked rice in the tub, spreading out in a layer, and sprinkle the sushi vinegar over a little by little. Using a spatula in a cut-and-turn motion, coat the grains in the sushi vinegar. Fan the rice gently to cool down to room temperature and continue folding the vinegar mixture into the rice until it begins to look glossy but don't over-mix.

Add the asparagus stalk pieces and sugar snaps into the sushi rice and mix evenly. Divide the rice mixture into four individual serving dishes, scatter the scrambled egg on top and garnish with the asparagus tips and halved tomatoes. Sprinkle over the sesame seeds to serve.

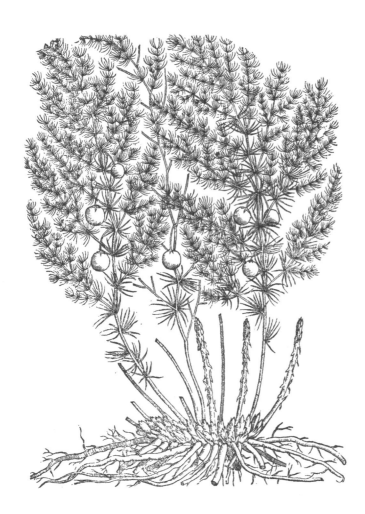

Chetna Makan

Red kidney beans and potato curry:
Rajma alu curry

A lot more people are giving red kidney beans a chance, whether in a curry, stew, salad or burgers. I love a red kidney bean curry or as we call it *rajma* and usually soak the beans overnight, cooking it next morning slowly until its super soft and cooked. Clearly that is not possible when trying to put a curry together in 30 minutes and that's the time to go for the tinned goods. And cooked with potatoes and spices this could become a curry you make again and again.

Vegan
Serves 4

2 tbsp sunflower oil
1 tsp cumin seeds
10 fresh curry leaves
2 onions, finely chopped
2 garlic cloves, grated
2.5cm ginger, grated
2 tomatoes, finely chopped
1 tsp salt
1 tsp garam masala
1 tsp chilli powder
1 tsp turmeric powder
2 tsp ground coriander
1 potato, cut into small cubes
2 x 400g tin of red kidney beans
handful of fresh coriander

Heat the oil in a pan and add the cumin seeds and curry leaves and when they start to sizzle add the onions. Cook these for 6 minutes on medium heat until lightly golden. Now add the ginger and garlic and cook for another minute.

Add the tomatoes and mix well. Cover and cook on medium heat for 5 minutes. Now is the time when you add all the spices and mix well. Then add the potato and the beans with 300ml of boiling water.

Cover and cook on medium heat for 15 minutes, stirring half way through. Finish with coriander leaves and serve with some rice or paratha. If you have time let it cook for longer, maybe 30 or 40 minutes on low heat.

Tom Hunt

Emmer wheat salad with apricots, broad beans and seaweed

The brilliant orange apricots shine out against the dark, iron-rich seaweed in this colourful salad, which is bursting with a tangy fusion of different flavours. Emmer, also known as farro, is an ancient ancestor of durum wheat and was one of the first cereals to be cultivated by humans. It is very flavoursome and can be milled into flour to use in baking or added whole to soups, stews or salads. You could substitute it here with other grains like amaranth, fonio, millet, quinoa, rye, spelt or teff, incorporating other seasonal fruit or vegetables to make endless colourful combinations. Nutrition-dense grains like these take a little while to boil. Consider cooking up a bulk batch to save energy. They keep well in the fridge for up to 5 days in an airtight container and can be used to replace rice, potato or carbohydrates in any meal or salad.

Vegan

Serves 2 as a main meal, 4–6 as a side dish

150g emmer wheat or other grain

80g Brazil nuts (or other nuts)

2 tbsp maple syrup or other sweetener

200g broad beans (podded weight, about 500g pods)

8 apricots, halved, stoned and then torn into large pieces

6g hijiki seaweed (or other seaweed), soaked for 10 minutes in cold water and then drained

60g bean sprouts

5 mint sprigs, leaves picked, stalks finely chopped

4 parsley sprigs, leaves roughly chopped, stalks finely chopped

2 tbsp extra virgin olive oil

1 unwaxed lemon, zest and juice

marigold petals or other edible flowers, to serve (optional)

Place the emmer wheat (or other grain) in a medium pan, cover with three times the quantity of water and bring to the boil. Simmer for 1–1½ hours, covered, until cooked through, but still chewy, topping up the water as necessary. Drain and set aside to cool.

Toast the nuts in a dry pan over a medium heat until they are lightly toasted. Stir in 1 tbsp of the maple syrup and season with a pinch of salt. Remove from the heat and set aside.

Taste the broad beans. If they are tender enough, leave them raw. If they are tougher, blanch them in a large pan of salted boiling water for a minute and then drain.

Combine all of the ingredients in a serving bowl, setting aside half of the nuts, apricots, seaweed and flower petals and then sprinkle these over the finished salad.

Rachel Roddy
Braised lentils with pan-fried porcini

I've read many descriptions of porcini (which means little pigs), the best, though, is that of Alan Davidson, in his *Oxford Companion to Food*, who compares the bulbous stem to a champagne cork and the colour of the cap to a glazed bun. Their cost of course, is closer to champagne than buns, good job one or two go a long way. Like a good steak, or any good ingredient, really, porcini are best cooked and served simply. While smaller, fresh porcini can be served raw (sliced paper-thin and dressed with olive oil and maybe some crystal shards of Parmesan), it is heat that brings out the rich flavour and curious, almost custardy texture of the cap. I like them sliced and grilled (in a ridge or hot cast-iron pan) or *trifolati*, that is cooked over a lively flame with oil, garlic and parsley, and eaten just so. Or with lentils, braised Roman style, with a soffritto of extra virgin olive oil, onion, carrot, celery and garlic. In Rome, they say lentils bring fortune. It is the magic of their form. Shaped (a bit) like coins, lentils are an augury of wealth and happiness: the more you eat, the better your fortune, to balance the fortune you have spent on porcini (field mushrooms work beautifully too).

Serves 4

For the lentils

4 tbsp extra virgin olive oil

1 medium onion, finely chopped

1 medium carrot, finely chopped

1 rib of celery, finely chopped

2 garlic cloves, finely chopped

300g small brown lentil

2 bay leaves

For the porcini

1 large or 2 medium porcini, or 250g field mushrooms

2 tbsp olive oil and a knob of butter

1–2 garlic cloves, peeled and gently crushed (split but still whole)

1 heaped tsp chopped parsley

salt and black pepper

Cover the base of a large, heavy-based frying or sauté pan with olive oil over a medium-low heat, add the chopped vegetables and cook gently until they are soft, but not coloured.

Pick over the lentils to check for grit, rinse and add them to the pan along with the bay leaves, stirring for a minute or two. Cover with 1.2 litres of water to about 2.5cm above the lentils, bring to the boil and reduce to a simmer. Cook the lentils, stirring occasionally, adding a little more water if needed, until they are tender, but not squidgy, and most of the liquid has been absorbed. This will take 25–50 minutes, depending on the lentils.

While the lentils cook, clean the mushrooms using a cloth or little knife to brush, scrape or pare away any grit or earth from the stalk, then use a damp cloth to wipe the stalk and cap. Cut the mushrooms into 2mm slices, cutting the cap and stem separately, if you prefer.

In a large frying pan, warm the oil and a little butter and the garlic, until the garlic is fragrant. Add the mushrooms, raise the flame and cook, stirring, for a few minutes until they absorb the fat, then reduce the flame and cook for 8–10 minutes, or until they are cooked through.

In the last 30 seconds, add salt, pepper and parsley, raise the heat and stir. Season the lentils with salt and pepper and divide between plates and top with porcini, remembering to pour any pan juices over the top.

Zaleha Kadir Olpin
Sticky rice bon bon: *pulut sambal*

This is a vegetarian version of a traditional savoury tea time snack. The creamy sticky rice complements the spicy and sweet tones of the coconut floss. This dish is also suitable for vegans.

Vegan

Serves 6

375g glutinous rice
250ml coconut milk
375ml water
2 tsp vegetable oil
¼ tsp salt
2 pandan leaves, rinsed and tied into a knot

Coconut floss

1 tbsp coriander seeds
½ tsp fennel seeds
½ tsp cumin seeds
¼ tsp black pepper powder
2 tbsp vegetable oil
175g desiccated coconut
½ tsp salt
1 tbsp sugar, or to taste

Spice paste for coconut floss

2 stalks lemon grass, white part only, roughly chopped
2 cloves garlic, peeled
150g shallots, peeled
1cm knob galangal, peeled
2 red chillies
125ml coconut milk

Soak the rice in water for 2 hours.

Drain the rice, then place in a rice cooker with the coconut milk, water, oil and salt. Stir to mix. Add the pandan leaves and turn the rice cooker on to cook. When the rice is done, fluff the rice using a fork and set it aside to cool.

Place the ingredients for the spice paste in a blender and process until smooth. Remove and set aside.

Prepare the coconut floss. Heat a dry pan over medium heat. Add the coriander seeds, fennel seeds, cumin seeds and black pepper and toast until fragrant. Remove and set aside.

Heat the oil in a pan over medium heat. Add the spice paste and fry until it is slightly dry and the oil separates.

Add the desiccated coconut, toasted spices, salt and sugar. Turn the heat down and keep stirring until the coconut is dry. Transfer to a bowl and set it aside to cool.

Take a tablespoonful of rice and roll it into a ball. Toss it in the coconut floss and coat well. Serve.

Dan Lepard
Marmalade wholegrain tart

A tart that celebrates the beautiful texture of wholegrains, merging the delicious Easter pastiera of Naples with Britain's Bakewell pudding and maids of honour, holding a filling that combines cooked barley, sweet fresh cheese and almonds with a dashing layer of your very best marmalade.

The maslin reference in the shortcrust here refers to an old English name for a flour mix that was made from rejected grains like rye, spelt, oats, once considered too unsophisticated for the grandest baking. Well, for me they give it grandeur, and the flavour they add to this all-butter shortcrust makes it ever so good to eat. Best made the day before so the marmalade has time to re-set and firm.

Serves 4–6
Makes one 18cm diameter tart

For the maslin shortcrust

120g strong white bread flour

50g wholemeal flour, or a mix of rye, spelt, oat flours

pinch salt

30g icing sugar

100g unsalted butter

one 60g egg

For the cheese and grain filling

60g pearl barley

80g cream cheese

80g curd cheese, like ricotta

100g ground almonds

80g caster sugar

½ tsp vanilla paste, or a few tsp of extract

finely grated zest of an orange

2–3 tsp whisky, malt if you like a smoky flavour

one 60g egg (you'll save a few tsp to brush the crust)

about 160g good marmalade, or a preserve you prefer

For the maslin shortcrust, put the flours, salt and sugar in a bowl. Rub in the butter with your fingers, then add the egg and mix well to a smooth and very soft paste. In truth it will seem unmanageably soft and paste-like but don't worry. Scoop it onto a piece of baking parchment or cling film, press it into a block about 2cm thick and chill in the fridge for an hour.

For the filling, put the pearl barley in a saucepan, cover with water, bring to the boil then simmer briskly for about 20 minutes until soft with still a touch of chew to it. Drain into a sieve, rinse with cold water, then drain again.

Place the cream cheese, curd cheese, ground almonds, sugar, vanilla, orange zest, whisky and egg (reserving a few teaspoons for brushing) in a bowl and beat everything together smoothly. Add the well-drained cooked barley and stir well.

Roll the pastry thinly and line the base and sides of a round fluted 18cm loose-base tart tin or similar. Spread the marmalade evenly over the base then spread the cheese and grain filling over that. Using leftover pastry, roll and cut strips to decorate the top in a lattice pattern, then brush the strips with the remaining beaten egg to make them shine. Heat the oven to 190°C/170°C fan and bake for about 50 minutes until the top is gently golden and the marmalade possibly starting to bubble up around the edges.

Remove from the oven and leave until very cold, or better still, the next day. Perfect dusted with a little icing sugar and served with a scoop of clotted cream.

Loder Valley Nature
Reserve, Wakehurst

Catherine Phipps
Mushroom *larb* with shiso leaves

Elisabeth Luard
Spinach and herb tortilla

Timothy d'Offay
Lightning leaf iced tea

Raymond Blanc
Chicory gratin

Da-Hae West
Vegan kimchi

Liz Knight
Nettle and dandelion omelette

LEAVES

Brwa Ahmad
Sautéed chard: *silqy swr*

Monica Galetti
Walnut and pear salad with a creamy Roquefort sauce

Carla Capalbo
Wild and cultivated greens with walnut paste: Georgian *pkhali*

Tessa Kiros
Baked stuffed vine-leaves: *dolmades*

Felicity Cloake
Perfect spanakopita

Helen Goh
Pandan chiffon cake

In the world of plants, leaves play an essential role. Plants with green leaves are autotrophic, meaning that they create their own food. To do this, plants carry out a process called photosynthesis, in which they use sunlight, water and carbon dioxide to create sugars which give them energy with which to grow. Leaves are integral to this, as they gather in sunlight. Chlorophyll, the pigment which gives leaves their green colour, absorbs the light and the process of photosynthesis takes part in leaves. Human beings, in turn, have fed on leaves for thousands of years, first finding them in the wild, then learning how to cultivate leafy plants as a food source. After the long, cold, dark days of winter, one can imagine how welcome the first young leaves of spring were. In many countries gathering wild leaves remains part of the food culture to this day, as in Greece's *horta* (meaning 'wild greens'), a dish of leafy wild greens, boiled or steamed and dressed with olive oil and lemon juice. In Britain, the revival of an interest in foraging is making a new generation aware of the abundance of edible leaves to be found in our fields, hedgerows and forests.

As the phrase 'eat your greens' implies, leaves play an important role in our diet, providing us with essential nutrients such as the vitamins A and K, and fibre. Leafy plants are also rich in phytonutrients (plant nutrients) which may prove beneficial to human health. Cruciferous vegetables such as brussels sprouts, cabbage and kale, are high in glucosinolates (in effect, a component of the plant's chemical defence system) and research is being carried out into their possible anti-cancer properties.

We grow and eat a variety of leaves from different plant families. Over human history, wild leafy plants – often intensely bitter – were cultivated and grown for traits we valued. Lettuce – that iconic salad vegetable – has a long history of human use. A plant resembling lettuce is depicted in Ancient Egyptian art. The Greeks and Romans cultivated lettuce, with the latter attributing it with soporific qualities. Today we enjoy a range of greens from the lettuce family, including lettuces, radicchio, puntarella, chicory and dandelion. The brassica family (Brassicaceae) includes kale, rocket and cabbages, and other important leafy vegetables which we enjoy in numerous forms. The Chinese cabbage, indigenous to East Asia, has been cultivated in China since the 5th century. In Europe too, the cabbage has been cultivated for several centuries and has long been a staple vegetable.

As we all know, once picked, leaves wilt very quickly. With freshness key to enjoying leaves at their very best, having a go at growing your own culinary leaves is well worth a try. Leafy crops – from lettuce to spinach – can be grown successfully in containers, so you don't need a large amount of land. Cut and come again plants – such as amaranth, Japanese greens, rucola and sorrel – are rewarding to grow and the continual harvesting helps avoid the risk of having a glut. Leafy crops can be tricky to germinate *in situ* as they have very small seeds and so need soil with a very fine tilth. For the best results, Hélèna Dove, Kew's kitchen gardener, recommends starting them off in modules, then subsequently transplanting.

We use leaves in several different ways in the kitchen – in the form of herbs to bring flavour and aroma, as an edible wrapping for fillings, added to braises, stews or curries, blended into smoothies or fermented to form richly flavourful sauerkraut or kimchi. Many of the leaves we eat have a fragile structure and this is reflected in the cooking methods we use in order not to overcook them, such as blanching, wilting or stir-frying, where the contact with heat is brief. And, of course, the most fundamental way of eating many leaves is to serve them raw, simply tossing them with a dressing and enjoying them as a salad. The sheer beauty of leaves – the different shapes and colours in which they come – makes them a very special and pleasurable ingredient.

As part of Kew's work looking to ensure sustainable plant food sources for the future in the face of climate change, Kew is researching chaya (*Cnidoscolus aconitifolius*), a fast-growing, leafy shrub native to the Yucatán Peninsula of southern Mexico. Also known as tree spinach, chaya is valued for being nutritious, as it is rich in protein, vitamins A, B and C, iron, calcium and potassium. However, as the leaves also contain hydrocyanic acid, they must be cooked before eating. Chaya can be grown easily from cuttings in poor, sandy soil and is noted for being pest-resistant and tolerant of both heavy rain and drought.

Another initiative, the Adapting Agriculture to Climate Change Project, also known as the Crop Wild Relatives Project, led by the Crop Trust and Kew's Millennium Seed Bank, seeks to help plant breeders 'climate proof' agriculture by developing more resilient crops to feed both humans and livestock. To do this, attention focused on wild relatives of crops (the undomesticated wild cousins of our crops), which thrive in more challenging conditions than their cultivated counterparts. While often regarded as weeds, these crop wild relatives are hardy survivors and retain important genetic characteristics that can be harnessed to breed new crop varieties. Upon analysis, it became clear that many crop wild relatives had not been collected and stored in seed banks. Furthermore, many of these wild relatives are disappearing from their natural habitats, due to pressures such as deforestation, intensive grazing, the spread of intensive agriculture and urbanisation. It was important to act fast to collect their seeds and preserve their genetic diversity and the potential it offers to plant breeders. Seed collecting by partner institutes took place in 25 countries around the world from 2013–2018. In total, 4,644 unique seed samples representing 371 different species (or subspecies) of wild relatives of 28 important crops were collected. Among them were 356 samples of wild relatives of alfalfa (*Medicago sativa*), a high-yielding and nutritious animal fodder. Known as the 'queen of forages', alfalfa is particularly important for subsistence farmers living in areas with poor soil, where owning a healthy cow, sheep or goat can ensure food and income security. These crop wild relative seeds are now stored in seed banks around the world and at the Millennium Seed Bank, where they will be a valuable resource to plant breeders, researchers and farmers in helping to breed crops that have the resilience needed to cope with climate change and provide sustainable food for the future.

Beetroot growing in the
Kew kitchen garden

Catherine Phipps
Mushroom *larb* with shiso leaves

I often find myself confounded by the myriad flavours that I taste in shiso leaves. I detect something different every time – sometimes the floral, spicy notes of mint, basil and cinnamon are the most pronounced, sometimes I can taste blackcurrant.

Green shiso in particular has a deep note of peanut about it that is almost meaty; the red shiso in contrast has a Szechuan-esque lift to it, providing that mouth-tingling freshness. Consequently, it isn't always easy to figure out what to pair with them. The savouriness of this larb works really well, and I suggest you try your first one without any of the garnishes so as not to mask it. I have started growing my own shiso and use their micro-leaves when very young – they add an extra intensity. Shiso leaves look like plump nettle leaves and have a similar texture. When eating raw, make sure they are fresh and not dry, or they will feel tickly in the mouth and throat. If you just have a few and would rather use them in the larb, use lettuce leaves for wrapping.

Vegan

Serves 4

1 tbsp basmati rice

2 tbsp groundnut oil

200g field mushrooms, finely chopped

2 garlic cloves, finely chopped

3cm piece ginger, peeled and finely chopped

1 tbsp light soy sauce

1 tbsp lime juice

1 tsp smooth peanut butter

4 spring onions, finely chopped

2 tbsp peanuts, finely chopped

20–24 shiso leaves

For the garnishes (all optional)

a few coriander leaves

a few mint leaves

a few Thai basil leaves

baby shiso leaves or shredded salted shiso leaves

1 green chilli, finely chopped

Put a non-stick frying pan over a medium heat. When it is hot, add the rice and toast until it smells rich and nutty, then remove from the heat and cool. Crush lightly with a pestle and mortar and set aside.

Heat the oil in a large frying pan. When it is hot to the point that the air is shimmering above it, add the mushrooms, making sure they are well spread out – you need them to brown and crisp, not to wallow in a pool of their own making. Stir-fry for several minutes, then add the garlic and ginger. Mix the soy sauce with the lime juice and peanut butter until you have a smooth, runny paste, then pour this over the mushrooms. Continue to cook until there is no visible liquid in the pan. Remove from the heat and stir in the spring onions, peanuts and toasted rice.

Arrange on a platter with any of the garnishes and the shiso leaves. Eat by piling a spoonful onto a shiso leaf and eating in one mouthful.

Elisabeth Luard
Spinach and herb tortilla

Any soft-leaf herbs – parsley, chives, mint, tarragon, wild garlic, sorrel leaves, watercress, spring onion tops – are all possible inclusions for this fresh-flavoured Spanish omelette. This is a basic recipe that suits any combination of fresh veg with a leafy green – peas, broad beans, green or runner beans, diced asparagus, slivers of artichoke heart – bearing in mind that the volume of veg should be roughly equal to that of the egg.

**Serves 4–6 as a tapa,
2 as a main course**

400g fresh spinach or chard leaves, de-stalked

4 large free range eggs

salt and pepper

pinch of grated nutmeg (optional)

a generous handful soft-leaf herbs, de-stalked and chopped

a few scraps of white feta-type cheese (optional)

2 tbsp olive oil

Rinse the spinach leaves and shake off excess water. Cook the leaves till they collapse – a couple of minutes – in a lidded pan in the water that clings to the leaves. Drain well, chop roughly and leave to cool a little. Fork up the eggs with salt, pepper and the optional nutmeg. Stir in the cooked spinach and chopped herbs, plus cheese, if using.

Heat a tablespoon of olive oil over a gentle heat in a small frying pan, diameter 18–20cm. Tip in the egg-mixture. As soon as the edges begin to set, use a fork to pull the sides to the middle. Turn down the heat (unlike a French omelette, Spanish tortillas are cooked gently), lid loosely and cook for 5–6 minutes, occasionally neatening the edges with a fork or spatula, till the top begins to look set. Place a plate over the pan – it should completely cover it – and reverse the whole thing so the tortilla ends up soft-side down on the plate. Be brave – it's easy, just look out for hot oil drops.

Reheat the pan with a little more oil and return the tortilla to the pan, cooked-side up. Don't cover but continue to neaten the edges to form a pancake at least two fingers-width thick. It'll only need a couple more minutes to brown the underside. Don't overcook as you need it to stay juicy inside. Slip it out onto to a warm plate. Pat with kitchen paper to absorb excess oil.

Serve warm or at room-temperature, never cold from the fridge. To serve as a tapa, cut into bite-sized cubes. To share between two, cut into quarters. Bread and wine to accompany, as is natural in Spain.

Timothy d'Offay
Lightning leaf iced tea

Tea's journey from an obscure Chinese leaf to the world's favourite beverage has probably been due to its ability to be easily transported and then swiftly transformed into a delicious drink. As tea has travelled around the globe it has been brewed differently by almost every culture it has encountered, so tea can be a green foam in a big black bowl, a sweet spicy treat in a terracotta cup or a refreshing chilled drink served in a glass with a slice of lemon. Traditionally, the British have gravitated towards hot milky tea with sugar or sugary cakes and biscuits, but our tea tastes are changing as people discover new teas on their travels and better bottled tea. As freshly made iced tea is always better than something you can buy bottled, here's an easy recipe for hot summer days or when you want a healthy soft drink in a hurry.

Vegan
Serves 1

6–8g of your preferred leaf tea

This method is the fastest way to make a glass of tasty iced tea whenever you want.

Put 6–8g of your preferred leaf tea into a teapot.

Pour about 100ml of water over the leaves being careful to use 90°C water for a black tea and 70°C water for a green tea.

After 10 seconds of infusing the tea, pour off all the liquid tea off the leaves.

Add several ice cubes to the tea leaves in the teapot and some ice cubes to the glass you will drink from.

Add 200–250ml of cold tap water to the teapot and brew the tea for about a minute or longer if you want something stronger and then strain into the glass with the ice.

Raymond Blanc
Chicory gratin

A beloved classic of Belgian cooking; this is a simple, rustic family dish. The Comté cheese, which is from my home region, can be replaced by any British cheese.

Serves 2

For the chicory

4 heads yellow chicory

1 tbsp lemon juice

1 tbsp sugar

2 large pinches sea salt

6 white peppercorns

600ml water

For the chard

100ml water

10g unsalted butter

2 small Swiss chard stalks with leaves, chop the stalks into 1cm pieces; roughly chop the leaves

For the cheese sauce

35g unsalted butter

35g plain flour

450ml whole milk

100g Comté cheese, finely grated

1 tbsp Dijon mustard

pinch sea salt

pinch freshly ground white pepper

To assemble the gratin

50g Comté cheese, finely grated

To cook the chicory, place in a medium saucepan with the lemon juice, sugar, salt and peppercorns and add enough of the water to barely cover. Place on a medium heat, cover with a cartouche and a lid smaller than the diameter of the pan (this is to keep the chicory submerged) and bring to the boil. Reduce the heat and simmer for 45–60 minutes. It is important to cook the chicory slowly to remove most of its bitterness. Turn off the heat, lift the chicory on to a wire rack to cool and allow the moisture to escape. Once cool, gently press out any extra moisture with a tea towel.

Preheat the oven to 190°C/170°C fan.

To cook the chard stalks, put the water and butter into a medium saucepan on a high heat. Cook the chard stalks for 20 minutes, adding more water if necessary. Once tender, lift out the stalks and cook the leaves for 3 minutes. Strain, mix the stalks and leaves and arrange in a small gratin dish.

While the chard is cooking, make the cheese sauce. In a small saucepan on a medium heat, melt the butter. Add the flour, whisk until smooth and cook to a nutty blond colour. Take the pan off the heat, whisk in the milk and return to a medium heat. Cook for a further 4 minutes, stirring constantly with the whisk until the sauce thickens. It is important to cook it for at least 4 minutes as the starch needs this time to swell, which thickens the sauce. Add the cheese and mustard and cook for 3 minutes, stirring, until the cheese has fully melted. Remove from the heat, taste and adjust the seasoning if required.

To assemble the gratin, pack the chicory heads tightly in the gratin dish, then spoon over the cheese sauce, sprinkle with the Comté cheese. Bake in the top part of the oven for 25 minutes. The top is the hottest part of the oven and the air circulation will help ensure your gratin gains its wonderful golden-brown colour.

Da-Hae West
Vegan kimchi

Kimchi is Korea's best-known export and has seen a huge boom in popularity due to its immune boosting health properties and addictive spicy, tangy flavour. It was first created as a way of preserving vegetables and nutrients during the cold, harsh Korean winters, but now it has become an essential part of Korean cuisine – much more than a side dish and eaten at every meal. Kimchi is traditionally made with fermented shrimps and/or fish sauce but this vegan version makes kimchi more accessible and is just as delicious.

Vegan

Makes approx. 1 litre jar of kimchi

For the brine
1 Chinese cabbage, approx. 800g
50g salt

For the stock
500ml water
100g mooli
3 dried shiitake mushrooms
1 sheet of kelp, roughly cut
½ onion, peeled
2 spring onions

For the kimchi 'glue'
150ml cooled stock
1 tbsp sweet rice flour
4 tbsp gochugaru (Korean red pepper flakes)
2 spring onions, roughly chopped
1 carrot, julienned
2 tsp minced garlic
2 tsp minced ginger
1 apple, finely sliced (skin on)
2 tbsp light soy sauce

Brining
Remove the tough outer leaves and any remaining stalks from the base of the cabbage.

Cut a slit at the bottom of the cabbage, about 10cm above the stem and then split the cabbage by gently pulling apart from the cut. This helps to keep the leaves whole without shredding them. Do the same to each half again, so that each cabbage is quartered.

Rinse the cabbage quarters under water to get them wet so that the salt sticks to them, shaking off any excess water. For each cabbage quarter, take a small handful of salt and rub it up and down each leaf, making sure to particularly salt the parts closer to the stems as these leaves are thicker and then place them into a large clean container.

Leave to brine for 3 hours, turning each cabbage quarter every 30 minutes to make sure the salty water gets inside to season each leaf.

Stock
Bring all the stock ingredients to the boil. Reduce the heat to a simmer, and leave for 20 minutes. Strain the stock and leave to cool.

Kimchi glue
Whisk the sweet rice flour into 150ml of the cooled stock.

Add the remaining kimchi 'glue' ingredients and mix thoroughly; this is easiest done by hand (wear gloves!).

For the kimchi
After 3 hours of brining, thoroughly wash the cabbage in cold, running water to get rid of excess salt and any sediment between the leaves.

Using the same technique as the salting earlier, take a small handful of the kimchi glue and stuff the mixture into the thicker parts of the cabbage, rubbing each leaf up and down with the kimchi glue, to make sure that every leaf is thoroughly coated.

For each quarter, roll the top third of the cabbage into itself and wrap the largest outer leaf around it to form a little parcel.

Pack the kimchi parcels tightly into a large container (a clip lock food box or large jar works well) and scrape in any leftover kimchi glue to fill any gaps. This will help prevent any mould. However, make sure that there is space at the top of the container, as it will need some room to ferment and expand.

Leave at room temperature for 3–4 days to ferment and then, after this, move to the fridge. The kimchi will then continue to ferment but at a much slower rate, so every day it'll taste a little sharper and a little tangier. Kimchi is best eaten on the day of making it (where it is like a spicy, salty salad) or after 2 weeks once fermentation has fully taken place. If using kimchi as an ingredient for other recipes (e.g. kimchi pancakes, kimchi dumplings or kimchi fried rice), always use kimchi that is properly fermented and which has a tangy, sour taste.

Inside the Temperate House

Inside the Temperate House

Liz Knight
Nettle and dandelion omelette

Although many gardeners view them with contempt, nettles and dandelions have been part of human diets for thousands of years, and both are equal contenders for the ultimate superfood crown. Not only are these most common of 'weeds' highly nutritious, rich in vitamins and minerals, they both also contain antioxidants and anti-inflammatories in quantities that conventional farmed plants can only dream of.

The sting of nettles hides a beautiful, complex flavour, iron rich yet almost sweet. Dandelions have a more bitter character and a couple of leaves chopped into a dish like this omelette provides the perfect hint of bitter in an otherwise umami-laced dish. Nettles and dandelions are traditionally gathered in the spring, but they have a second flush of tender growth in the autumn and are delicious and fortifying as the days both lengthen and shorten. Make sure you gather both leaves from unpolluted, clean ground and only gather nettles before they have become leggy and produced flowers.

20g butter
1 clove of garlic, peeled
¼ white onion, finely chopped
30g nettle tops
1 large dandelion leaf
a pinch of salt
3 eggs
10g grated Parmesan cheese

Place the butter and the clove of garlic in a heavy-based frying pan and gently warm until the butter is melted. After a couple of minutes, remove the garlic, add the finely chopped onion and cook until the onion has softened but not browned.

Place the washed, still damp, nettle tops and dandelion leaf into the frying pan, sprinkle with salt, cover with a lid and leave on a low heat for a couple of minutes until the leaves have wilted. The nettle sting will be destroyed by heat.

Take off the heat and turn the buttery leaves and onions onto a chopping board, leaving as much butter as possible in the frying pan. Crack the eggs into a bowl with the Parmesan, and lightly beat to break up the egg and incorporate the cheese.

Chop the dandelion, nettle and onion until the leaves are in very small pieces, but not so small they become mushy.

Return the buttery pan to the heat and heat through. Pour in the egg and using a fork, pull the mixture a couple of times from the edges of the pan. Once the bottom of the omelette is cooked, pour over the chopped leaves, and keep on the heat until the top of the omelette starts to become opaque. Flip the omelette in half to seal in the nettle and dandelion and serve at once.

Brwa Ahmad
Sautéed chard: *silqy swr*

Growing up in a little village in Kurdistan, where this dish is a staple, I remember running around my mother while she was cooking this dish over a wood fire pit with a lot of smoke. I would grab little pieces of bread, dip them in the sauce and run away eating them.

My mother would often use different grains and pulses in this dish such as lentils, barley, or Khorasan grains, but they take much longer to cook. I have used puffed millet grains because they are sustainable, gluten-free, protein-rich and add a deliciously crunchy, textured element.

Vegan

Serves 4

1 tbsp rapeseed oil

100g shallots, roughly chopped

2 cloves of garlic, minced

1 bunch of Swiss chard chopped (reserve a little for garnish)

70g chopped tomatoes

1 tbsp tomato purée

100ml vegetable stock

salt and pepper

1 tsp cumin powder

50g puffed millet grains

In a heavy-based pan, heat the oil. Add the shallot and garlic and sauté for 5 minutes.

Add the chard and cook for 5 minutes, stirring now and then, until wilted.

Add the chopped tomatoes, tomato purée and vegetable stock, season, and add the cumin.

Cook for about 15 minutes or until the stock has reduced and thickened.

Top with puffed millet grains and some finely chopped chard.

Monica Galetti
Walnut and pear salad
with a creamy Roquefort sauce

**Serves 2 as a lunch
or 4 as a starter**

Caramelised pears

3 firm, ripe Conference pears

1 tbsp granulated sugar

25g salted butter

100ml sherry vinegar,
plus a little extra for the
dressing if needed

Salad

1 white chicory bulb, trimmed

1 red chicory bulb, trimmed

1 gem lettuce

30g rocket leaves

2 tbsp chopped chives

1 tsp walnut oil

1 tbsp olive oil

100g walnut halves

50g pickled walnuts

sea salt and freshly ground
black pepper

Roquefort sauce

150ml double cream

100g Roquefort, cut into pieces

Heat the oven to 180ºC/160ºC fan. For the sauce, put the cream and Roquefort in a saucepan and heat gently until the cheese has partially melted (there should be some small chunks); don't let it boil. Remove from the heat and set aside.

Peel, halve and core the pears, then cut into thick wedges. Scatter the sugar in a non-stick ovenproof pan and heat gently until melted, then cook to a light golden caramel. Add the pear wedges and toss to coat in the caramel. Add the butter and allow to met, then stir the sherry vinegar into the buttery caramel. Spoon the caramel sauce over the pears until they are well coated and golden, then transfer the pan to the oven and cook until the pears are soft, about 5 minutes.

Meanwhile, for the salad, separate the chicory and lettuce into leaves and toss them with the rocket and chives in a large bowl. When the pears are ready, transfer them to a warm dish and set aside.

Using a fork, whisk the walnut and olive oils into the caramel sauce, then taste and add a little more vinegar if you think it is needed. Use this dressing to dress the salad leaves and season lightly with salt and pepper to taste.

Arrange the salad and caramelised pears in a large shallow serving dish or on individual plates and sprinkle with the walnuts and pickled walnuts. Drizzle with the Roquefort sauce and serve at once.

Carla Capalbo
Wild and cultivated greens with walnut paste: Georgian *pkhali*

In the country of Georgia, in the Caucasus Mountains, foraging is as much a part of the culture as growing one's own vegetables. The beautiful rural landscape offers a wide array of fungi, flowers, nuts and leaves that the Georgians cook and preserve. The blossoms of the black locust tree (*Robinia pseudoacacia*) and Caucasian bladdernut bush (*Staphylea colchica*) are salt-fermented for use as pickles. Walnuts are pounded into sauces using pestle and mortar and flavoured with the dried petals of French marigold (*Tagetes patula*), garlic and aromatic herbs. Wild and bitter greens – from dandelion and nettles to field greens and *ekala*, the tender shoots of greenbrier (*Smilax*) – are cooked, cooled and mixed with walnut paste for a delicious, nutritious starter. The Georgians shape them into leaves and circles, topped with coriander or pomegranate seeds. For this recipe use any edible wild greens you can find, plus spinach, chard and/or beet greens.

Vegan
Serves 4–6

For the walnut paste
150g walnut halves
3 garlic cloves, or more to taste
½ tsp coriander seeds, crushed
¼ tsp ground blue fenugreek, optional
1 tsp dried marigold petals, optional
1 tsp salt
1 tbsp chopped mint
3 tbsp chopped coriander leaves
1 tsp minced dill
fresh chilli, to taste
75ml water

For the leaves
600g leafy greens (see list above)
120ml water
1 tbsp lemon juice or white wine vinegar
2 tbsp finely chopped coriander
1 tbsp finely chopped parsley
salt and black pepper
pomegranate seeds, for decoration

Make the walnut paste: combine all the ingredients in the bowl of a food processor and pulse until you have an even paste. Some people prefer a more granular mixture while others like a smoother texture: there are no rigid rules. Turn the paste into a small bowl and cover tightly with clingfilm. Refrigerate until ready to use. This recipe will make more than you need for the *pkhali*; refrigerate or freeze the rest for use with other vegetables or as a sauce for dipping, loosed with a little pomegranate juice.

Thoroughly wash the leaves in several changes of cold water until all the grit has been removed. Shake off the excess water and chop roughly.

Push all the greens into a saucepan with 120ml water. Cook, covered, stirring occasionally, until they wilt down and are cooked to your preference. When cool enough to handle, squeeze the greens with your hands to remove the excess liquid. (Save a few tablespoons of the cooking water.) Chop the greens very finely.

Mix a few tablespoons of the walnut paste with the lemon juice or vinegar and chopped herbs. If the sauce is very thick, stir in a spoonful of the reserved cooking liquid.

Mix the greens with the walnut sauce. Taste for seasoning. Form into small balls or leaf shapes and decorate with pomegranate seeds. Serve cool or at room temperature.

The Mediterranean Garden

Tessa Kiros
Baked stuffed vine-leaves: *dolmades*

This is a lovely and more unusual version than you might find readily available in Greece. The *dolmades* are fun to make with people helping – as the Greeks do – all sitting at the table. It is easy to double the amount and have enough for the next day too – just use a bigger baking dish. I like to serve them with a dish of thick sheep's yoghurt – with a little salt scattered into it – or tzatziki, on the side.

Makes about 40

about 40 good vine-leaves

250g mushrooms

200g courgettes

1 carrot, peeled

3 large ripe tomatoes

1 red onion, peeled and chopped

1 Greek coffee cup of olive oil (6–7 tbsp)

2 cloves garlic, peeled and chopped

180g medium-grain rice

½ tsp ground cinnamon

3 tbsp each chopped fresh parsley, dill and mint

½ tbsp dried mint

juice of 1 lemon

3 tbsp grated kefalotiri or Parmesan cheese

thick yoghurt for serving

If using bottled leaves, rinse them in cold water. Drain, pat dry with paper towels then stack in piles and keep aside.

Using the large holes of a grater, grate the mushrooms, courgettes, carrot into a bowl. Halve the tomatoes and grate those into a separate bowl – so the skin stays behind in your hand.

Sauté the onion in a couple of tablespoons of the oil in a wide pot until pale golden. Add the garlic and sauté until it smells good. Add the mushrooms, carrots, zucchini, the rice and cinnamon and sauté for about 10 minutes on a gentle heat. Add half of the grated tomato, the fresh herbs, dried mint and lemon juice. Season with salt and pepper and simmer for another 5 minutes. Remove from the heat and stir in the kefalotiri.

Preheat the oven to 180'°C/160°C fan. Spread a few whole vine-leaves at a time on your work surface, shiny side down. Trim away the stem, then spoon a heaped tablespoon of filling onto each leaf and roll up neatly and snugly, tucking in the sides after the first roll, then continuing to roll. I find it easy to divide my mixture with a spoon into four, so I can judge the filling amounts better. Smaller leaves will need less filling. Have a large round baking dish ready. If you have a few torn leaves, lay them at the bottom and sides of the baking dish. Arrange the *dolmades* fairly tightly in concentric circles to make one layer (if they don't all fit, then you can stack a few on top). Scatter the rest of the tomato over the tops of the *dolmades*. Add 250ml of water and drizzle over the remaining oil. Sprinkle with a little salt and pepper. Rock the dish two or three times to distribute the liquid. Cover with foil. Bake for an hour, then uncover. Add another 250ml or so of water and bake for 10 minutes more – they should be just a little roasted and still moist.

Remove from the oven, let them cool down a little, then serve warm, or at room temperature (some love them cold) with salted yoghurt on the side.

Felicity Cloake
Perfect spanakopita

This spinach pie is a Greek classic: sweet, earthy leaves and salty cheese encased in layers of shatteringly crisp pastry, it's as good for breakfast as it is for lunch or dinner. Being delicious hot or cold, vegetarian-friendly and fairly cheap to put together, it's also an excellent choice for a picnic and, should you wish to make it in little triangles or cigars rather than one large pie, finger food of the highest order. In short, if you don't have one already, you need a recipe for spanakopita in your life. (Note you can substitute just about any quick-cooking leafy greens for spinach here, from nettles to watercress.) Recipe first published in *The Guardian*, in Felicity's *How to Make the Perfect* cookery column.

Makes 6–8 pieces

1kg adult spinach,
or frozen whole leaf spinach,
defrosted

salt

1 red onion or leek,
finely chopped

2 tbsp olive oil

4 spring onions, chopped

300g feta, crumbled

25g dill, chopped

20g mint, leaves removed and chopped

3 sprigs oregano, chopped

50g bulgur wheat (optional)

2 eggs, beaten

zest of 1 unwaxed lemon

nutmeg

250g filo pastry

oil, to brush

Trim the spinach and wash well, then roughly chop. Put in a colander with a good sprinkle of salt, and massage until it wilts (omit this stage if using frozen).

Gently fry the red onion or leek in the oil until softened, then take off the heat and stir in the spring onion. Tip into a large bowl with the feta, herbs and bulgur, if using.

Wring the spinach in handfuls until no more liquid comes out (it should look thoroughly wilted), stir into the cheese mix, then add the egg, lemon zest, a glug of oil and a good grating of nutmeg and mix again (I find hands the best tool for this). Season lightly, remembering that feta is quite salty.

Heat the oven to 200°C/180°C fan. Brush a roughly 30cm x 25cm baking tin with olive oil, then line with half the filo, brushing each sheet with oil as you go (a spray is useful here, if you have one), and taking care not to press them down in the process. Leave any excess overhanging the sides.

Spoon in the filling, level the top, then, to put the lid on, repeat the layering process with the remaining pastry. Fold the overhang inwards to make an edible rim, drizzle with more oil and cut into the desired portion sizes.

Bake for about 30–40 minutes, until golden. Leave to cool slightly or completely before serving.

Helen Goh
Pandan chiffon cake

Pandan, or screwpine are long blades of leaves used widely in South East Asia to impart a subtle but distinct flavour to both savoury and sweet dishes. The leaves may be knotted and used to infuse rice or pudding mixes, or to wrap morsels of food before grilling or frying. Here, the green juice is extracted by blending with coconut milk to flavour this delightfully light and billowy chiffon cake.

Serves 10–12

150ml thick coconut milk

8 pandan leaves, cut into roughly 3–4 cm pieces

7 eggs, yolks and whites separated

300g caster sugar, divided

90ml oil (flavourless and colourless is best)

1 tsp vanilla extract

150g self-raising flour

1 tsp cream of tartar

⅛ tsp salt

icing sugar for dusting on top

Preheat oven to 180°C/160°C fan. You will also need a 23cm tube/chiffon cake tin with a removable base, and which is *not* non-stick.

Combine the coconut milk and pandan leaves in a blender and blend on low speed for about a minute, then increase the speed to medium-high and continue blending until the pandan leaves are crushed and the milk is tinged green. Strain the pandan milk through a fine sieve placed over a medium bowl. Use a spatula or spoon to press on the crushed leaves to extract as much of the liquid as possible, then discard the green pulp. Set aside for the time being.

In a large mixing bowl, combine the egg yolks and half of the sugar (150g) and whisk together until light and creamy. Add the oil, vanilla and strained pandan milk. Whisk until well combined, then sift the flour, ½ tsp cream of tartar and salt directly into the mix. Whisk to incorporate, then set the bowl aside for now.

Place the egg whites in the bowl of a cake mixer fitted with the whisk attachment. Beat on high speed until frothy – about 30 seconds – then add the remaining ½ tsp cream of tartar. Continue to beat until soft peaks form, then gradually drizzle in the remaining 150g of sugar. Continue to whisk until stiff, glossy peaks form.

Using a large whisk or rubber spatula, gently fold about a third of the egg whites into the bowl with the pandan and egg yolk mixture. Use soft, wide movements with the whisk or spatula when folding – you want to be thorough, but not deflate the air bubbles. When almost incorporated, repeat with another third of the egg whites, then the final third. There should not be any egg whites visible, though some faint white streaks may remain.

▶▶

Scrape the batter into the *ungreased* chiffon tin and place into the oven. Bake for 55–60 minutes, or until a skewer inserted into the middle of the cake comes out clean. Remove from the oven and immediately invert the cake tin. Don't worry if the removable base slips down a little when the cake is turned over: the cake will still stay suspended because the tin is not greased. Set aside for about 1 hour, until completely cool.

To unmould the cake, turn the tin the right way up and using a long metal spatula, loosen the cake from the sides and base of the tin, as well as the central tube. Invert the cake back on to a serving plate. Dust the top of the cake lightly with icing sugar before serving.

Note

Once the cake comes out of the oven, the tin is turned upside-down to leave to cool completely. This is because the air bubbles trapped in the cake are heavy, and if left the right side up, the cake would collapse under its own weight. Turning it upside-down allows the cake to be suspended so that it cannot collapse, but only if the tin is *not* non-stick. If it is non-stick, the cake would fall out when turned upside-down to hold the air bubbles *in situ* until it cools and forms a firm structure.

The Agius Evolution Garden

Diana Henry
Roast pumpkin and tomatoes
with burrata and hazelnut pesto

Olia Hercules
Vegetarian borsch

Claire Thomson
Squash baked with beer, cheese, cream and pretzels

Vanessa Bolosier
Gratin d'igname: yam gratin

Simon Hopkinson
Potato pie with Beaufort cheese

ROOTS, SQUASHES AND TUBERS

**Sarit Packer and
Itamar Srulovich, Honey & Co**
Spicy pumpkin, quince and date stew

Zoe Adjonyoh
Yam and plantain peanut curry

Rosie Sykes
Parsnip and coconut cake

Anna Jones
Squash and crispy kale pizza

Martin Allen Morales
Oca with cashew and chipotle sauce

When it comes to edible plants, humans eat every part of them, including those which grow underground. Root vegetables and the thickened stems we call tubers, corms and rhizomes evolved as storage organs for plants. In them they keep the sugars created by photosynthesis in the form of carbohydrates. Human selection and breeding has significantly changed them in size, shape and edibility. Another group of plants which humans eat are squashes. These belong to the cucumber family (Cucurbitaceae), develop from a flower and contain seeds. In botanical terms they are a fruit, but more generally are considered to be vegetables. Starchy root and tuber crops are a major global source of carbohydrates after cereals, feeding not only humans but also livestock. While high in carbohydrates, calcium and vitamin C, they are low in protein. Potatoes, cassava and sweet potatoes make up 90 per cent of the global production of roots and tubers.

Originally from the Andes mountains of South America – where it was first cultivated – the potato (which is a stem tuber) is an important source of energy. From the culinary point of view, the mild-flavoured potato is a delightfully versatile vegetable, which can be baked, boiled, braised, fried or roasted. Classic potato dishes reflect its range of uses: finely sliced and baked in a gratin as in France's potato Dauphinoise, cooked with spices for India's *aloo dum* and – of course – sliced and deep-fried to make that perennial favourite, chips. The world of root vegetables, however, also offers many other delights: beetroot, carrots, celeriac, jicama, parsnip, taro, salsify, turnips and yam, to name just some. Each of these have their own flavour and can be eaten and enjoyed in a variety of ways.

Squashes vary in colour, shape and size, from small patty pans to huge, heavy pumpkins. Culinary squashes are often divided into two groups: summer squash and winter squash. Summer squashes can be harvested at an immature stage, when their skin is soft and once picked will only keep for a few weeks. Of this group, the courgette is the best known. Delicate in flavour and texture, they can be cooked in a variety of ways, including stuffing and baking, frying or in pasta sauces. Winter squashes – such as butternut or Delica pumpkin– are harvested when fully mature when their skin is hard and have the useful capacity of storing well. Valued for their nutritious qualities, winter squashes are noted for their natural sweetness of flavour. This means they lend themselves to use in both sweet and savoury dishes, such as America's much-loved pumpkin pie or Japan's simmered kabocha in dashi.

Growing your own root vegetables and squashes is possible even if space is limited. Potatoes, carrots and courgettes, for example, can all be grown successfully in deep containers of multi-purpose compost. When it comes to potatoes, choose which you want to grow – first earlies, second earlies and main crops (names which indicate when they will be ready to harvest) – and buy the relevant seed potatoes. Freshly harvested vegetables, picked a few minutes before cooking, have a wonderful depth of flavour.

Adapting agriculture to climate change to ensure food security is one of the urgent challenges of our time. Kew's work on the Crop Wild Relatives Project has conserved the seeds of the wild relatives of 29 crops, including the carrot, potato and sweet potato. The tragedy of the Irish Potato Famine, when potato blight had a devastating effect on Ireland's staple crop, is a sobering reminder of the perils posed by plant disease. Conserving seeds from crop wild relatives in seed banks is a vital step in potentially developing new disease resistant varieties.

One crop which scientists at Kew are researching with regard to food security is enset, a member of the banana family which is cultivated in Ethiopia. A staple crop there, it is called 'the tree against hunger'. Unlike the banana, it is the starchy stems and underground corm that are eaten rather than the fruit. The pulp of the corm and pseudostem is fermented for up to six months to make kocho which is used in dough to make bread. Bulla is a white, starchy powder, obtained when the scrapings and pulp used to make kocho are squeezed before fermentation and the resulting liquid and starch are separated. Bulla can be kept for years and is rehydrated with water to make dumplings, porridge, pancakes or a beverage. In the Southern Nations, Nationalities, and People's Region, bulla is mixed with traditional seasoned butter and spices, resulting in small grains which resemble couscous. Enset has several important food security traits. It grows in a variety of conditions, is somewhat drought-tolerant and can be harvested at any one time, between 3–7 year intervals. As well as being an important dietary starch source, it provides fibres, medicines, animal fodder, roofing and packaging and stabilises soils and microclimates. It can also be found growing in Kew's Temperate House.

Kew's work on researching and conserving resource-providing plants includes a project in Madagascar, the most economically impoverished country in the world that is not an active war zone. The project protects wild yams and promotes livelihoods. There are at least 45 wild yam species in Madagascar, many not found anywhere else. Wild and cultivated yam tubers are an important food, usually eaten boiled and providing carbohydrates, fibre, potassium and various micronutrients. Rural communities harvest wild yams, both for their own consumption and to sell to the island's more urban communities. They play a key role in people's diets in the late dry season – known as the 'hungry gap' – when other foods like rice have been used up. However at least 12 of these species are threatened by over exploitation, habitat loss and climate change. Kew is working with local communities to maintain a sustainable food supply for low-income families in the face of climate change. Kew research has shown that when the winged yam (*Dioscorea alata*) is cultivated more extensively by communities alongside wild species it improves food security and livelihoods, conserves species and reduces pressure in forests. Kew scientists believe that they have taken an important step towards sustainable management by Malagasy communities to protect their unique yams for use by future generations. It is an approach which is scalable and could help millions across Madagascar.

Freshly harvested beetroot
in the Kew kitchen garden

Diana Henry

Roast pumpkin and tomatoes with burrata and hazelnut pesto

This is soft in texture so you really need the crunch of the toasted hazelnuts on top, and some good toasted ciabatta or sourdough on the side. I like Crown Prince pumpkin if I can get it but butternut squash is widely available and dependably sweet.

Serves 6 as a starter or small plate

900g squash or pumpkin
5 tbsp olive oil
15g butter
9 plum tomatoes, halved
1 tbsp balsamic vinegar
½ tsp granulated sugar
400–500g burrata
halved, toasted hazelnuts for garnishing
toasted bread, to serve

For the pesto
80g parsley
100g toasted hazelnuts
juice of ½ lemon
1 clove garlic, peeled
100ml extra virgin olive oil
35g grated Parmesan cheese

Preheat the oven to 190°C/170°C fan.

Halve and deseed the squash or pumpkin. Cut into slices about 3cm thick at the thickest part and peel each slice (you will serve one to two per person).

Put 3 tbsp of the olive oil and all the butter in a shallow roasting tin and heat gently. Add the wedges of squash, turning over to coat, and season well.

Lie the tomatoes in another roasting tin in a single layer. Drizzle with the rest of the olive oil and the balsamic vinegar, sprinkle on the sugar and season.

Roast both trays for 35–40 minutes (the tomatoes might take a little longer), or until tender and slightly caramelised. Baste the squash pieces every so often while cooking. The tomatoes will become slightly shrunken.

For the pesto, whizz the parsley, hazelnuts, lemon juice, garlic and some seasoning into a food processor while adding the olive oil. Stir in the Parmesan and check for seasoning.

It will be quite thick, so add a little warm water until it becomes spoon-able.

Divide the pumpkin and tomatoes between six plates. Break up the burrata and divide it between the plates, then spoon some pesto on top.

Scatter with toasted hazelnuts, if using, and serve with toasted bread.

Olia Hercules
Vegetarian borsch

In Ukraine, a country bigger than France, there are as many borsch recipes as there are seasons, regions, families. It is however always a brothy soup, never a purée. It can be made using rich meat or fish stocks, and traditionally those would have been made during festivities wherever meat was in season (yes, meat eating has also been a very seasonal affair in the past). But historically vegetarian versions would have been made most often. The basis for the stock could include dried ceps, root vegetables or first wild herbs in spring like wild garlic, chickweed and sorrel.

Apart from the green spring borsch, all other varieties feature beetroot – used either raw or fermented (in kvass form) or both. Whatever the variety, borsch's flavour profile is always quite complex – it should be perfectly balanced – sweet, sour, salty, earthy and sometimes a little piquant from garlic (fresh or fermented) and even chilli. This version is not strictly traditional, it is an amalgamation of all the elements in vegetarian borsch recipes that I personally love. A 'mixed tape' of ingredients that make for a very pleasant borsch eating experience. This version can be cooked pretty much all year round, just leave red peppers out in winter, when they are not in season.

Vegan
Serves 4

For the stock
25g dried mushrooms
(ceps are best)
½ celeriac, peeled
2 carrots, scrubbed
1 medium onion, peeled
5 allspice berries
1 bay leaf
some parsley stalks

For the stock, cover the dried mushrooms in 200ml of hot water and let them stand while you prepare the vegetables.

Cut the celeriac into small dice, and do the same with the carrots.

Strain the mushroom liquid into a medium stock pot, leaving the sediment behind. Then rinse the rehydrated mushrooms and add them in too. Put the whole peeled onion into the pot along with the celeriac, carrot, allspice, bay leaf, parsley stalks. Cover with 1.5l cold water and bring to a simmer. Cook for about 30 minutes.

Meanwhile, cut the beetroot into matchsticks and chop its stalks and leaves finely.

Heat 2 tbsp of oil in a large, deep frying pan and add the diced onion. Add a generous pinch of sea salt and cook, stirring from time to time for about 5 minutes or until the onion softens and starts becoming golden. If at any point the pan becomes too dry, you can always add a splash of water and scrape at the bottom of the pan. Now add the carrots and cook for another 5 minutes or until the carrots edges too start caramelising gently.

For the broth

3 medium beetroots + their stalks and leaves if there are any

1 onion, diced

sea salt

1 medium carrot, coarsely grated

1 red pepper, thinly sliced (optional)

1 red chilli, bruised (optional)

400g ripe tomatoes or 1 tin of good quality tomatoes

200g new potatoes, halved or regular potatoes, chopped

1 tin red kidney beans

25g dill, chopped

3 garlic cloves, peeled and chopped

Add the beetroot and its stalks and leaves and cook for another 5 minutes, then add the red peppers and chilli, if using, and the tomatoes and let it all bubble off for a further 5 minutes. You want the tomato to reduce by a quarter, which will happen quicker if you are using fresh tomato pulp.

Remove the whole onion and parsley stalks from the stock and then scrape the beetroot mixture into the stock. Add the potatoes (I don't bother peeling mine). Drain the beans and add them in too. Give it a good stir, taste it and season well with sea salt. Bring to a simmer.

Reserve a little bit of the dill, and put the rest of it with the garlic into a pestle and mortar and give it a good grinding. You are looking for a rough paste. When the potatoes are ready (pierce one with a knife to test), add this green paste, mix it through and switch off the heat. Cover the borsch and let it stand for 5–10 minutes before serving. Make sure to taste it before serving, if it tastes underwhelming, chances are you didn't add enough salt. Don't be scared to season properly, add some more salt and it will bring the flavours right out!

It is rather good with a small spoonful of creme fraiche stirred through each individual serving, some extra dill sprinkled on top and a hunk of fresh crusty bread.

Claire Thomson
Squash baked with beer, cheese, cream and pretzels

Serves 6–8

1 x 1.5–2kg squash (such as Crown Prince), or use 2 smaller squash (such as acorn)

100g aged gruyère cheese, grated

100g Emmental cheese, grated

100g Reblochon cheese, finely chopped (or use Taleggio, Fontina, Raclette or Camembert)

1–2 cloves of garlic, very finely chopped

2 tsp plain flour (optional, to stabilize the cheese)

150g pretzels, bashed into large crumbs

100ml ale or beer (such as amber ales, Belgian beers, not too hoppy)

100ml double cream

salt and freshly ground black pepper

Preheat the oven to 180°C/160°C fan.

Cut the top off the squash to make a lid, then hollow out the seeds. Season the inside cavity with salt and plenty of freshly ground black pepper and place on a baking tray. Replace the lid loosely and bake the medium-size squash for about 1–1½ hours or small squash for 30–45 minutes, until tender when skewered.

Meanwhile, mix the cheeses together in a bowl and combine with the garlic, and the flour (if using). Increase the oven to 200°C/180°C fan. Remove the squash from the oven and put to one side, leaving it (or them) in the baking tray and removing the lid(s). Scrape any cooked flesh off the lid(s) and place it in the squash cavity along with a few of the pretzel pieces.

A little at a time, add in the cheese mixture, beer, pretzels and cream (a little of one, then another, then the next, and so on – and repeat), finishing with a good sprinkling of pretzel pieces and cheese. Put the lid(s) back on the squash. Carefully put the squash back into the hot oven on the tray and bake for 20–30 minutes, or until the fondue is melted and bubbling within.

Vanessa Bolosier
Gratin d'igname: yam gratin

If you're having Easter lamb roast in Guadeloupe or Martinique, nine times out of ten it will be served with yam gratin. It's just one of those things. Try this one and serve it with lamb.

Serves 4–6

1kg yam

salt and freshly ground black pepper

2 tbsp sunflower oil

1 onion, very finely chopped

1 spring onion, very finely chopped

2 sprigs parsley, very finely chopped

1 tbsp cornflour

350ml milk

100g Emmental cheese, grated

Preheat the oven to 180°C/160°C fan.

Peel the yam and cut into small chunks. Place in a pan of lightly salted boiling water and boil for 30 minutes, until tender. Drain and mash with a fork. Set aside.

Heat the oil in a saucepan, add the onion, spring onion and parsley and sauté for 2 minutes. Add the cornflour and stir, then gradually add the milk, stirring all the time until smooth. Add some pepper and a third of the cheese. Stir into the mashed yam, and add salt and pepper to taste.

Transfer the mash to a gratin dish. Sprinkle the remaining cheese over the top. Bake for 30 minutes, until golden, patched with brown. Serve hot.

Simon Hopkinson
Potato pie with Beaufort cheese

A most luxurious and rich dish, here, for that which is, essentially, nothing more than potatoes in pastry.

Serves 4

500g medium potatoes (Desiree, for preference), washed

salt and freshly ground pepper

100ml double cream

2 garlic cloves, lightly bruised

25–30g butter

375g ready-made puff pastry, in 2 equal sheets

75g Beaufort cheese, very thinly sliced

½ tsp thyme leaves

beaten egg, to glaze the pastry

Preheat the oven to 200°C/180°C fan. Steam (for preference) or boil the potatoes in salted water until tender, then cool and peel. Slice moderately thickly and put to one side.

Place the cream in a saucepan with the garlic, bring to the boil, then take off the heat, cover and leave to infuse.

Put a flat baking sheet into the oven. Lightly smear another one with some of the butter. Roll out one puff pastry sheet thinly, to a 2–3mm thickness, and lay it on the buttered baking sheet. Mark a circle on it, about 20cm in diameter. Cover the pastry round with half of the potatoes, arranging them in a slightly overlapping layer within the circle. Lightly season and cover with half the cheese and thyme leaves, adding a few flecks of butter. Repeat these layers. Brush the pastry edges with beaten egg.

Roll out the other sheet of pastry as above and then place over the filling. Clamp down the edges with your fingers and then trim to a round, using a flan ring that is slightly larger than 20cm as a guide.

Now, brush the pastry all over with egg and, using the tines of a fork, decorate the edge. Make a small hole in the centre of the pie, about 5mm in diameter. Remove the garlic from the cream and, using a small funnel, slowly pour the infused cream into the pie through the hole, allowing it to settle inside before adding more. Once it is quite clear that no more cream will fit, stop pouring; you may have a modicum left.

Slide the pie into the oven, onto the preheated baking sheet. Bake for about 20 minutes, then turn the oven setting down to 180°C/160°C fan. Continue cooking for a further 20 minutes, or until crisp and nicely puffed; if the pie is browning too quickly, cover loosely with a sheet of foil.

Let the pie stand for a good 10 minutes out of the oven before serving. Cut into wedges and eat with a crisp green salad or just on its own.

Sarit Packer and Itamar Srulovich, Honey & Co

Spicy pumpkin, quince and date stew

Something between a roast and a stew, (we were playing with names: a stoast? a strew?), this is a dish to steam up your kitchen windows on a cold winter day, to fill your belly and really stick to the ribs. All the season's heroes — citrus, quince, golden gourds— come together with some heat and spice from chilli, ginger, cinnamon and an abundance of garlic, as well as toffee-sweet dates in a dish that is colourful and heady. Serve with buttered brown rice and, just possibly, toasted pumpkin seeds on top. You won't want winter to end.

Vegan

A main for 4–6 (if you serve with some rice or cracked wheat)

a large pumpkin of your choice, about 2kg

2 quince, cored and cut into large chunks (you can use apples or pears instead; just add them at the last 20 minutes instead of the beginning)

3 tbsp olive oil

1 tsp flaky sea salt

1 cinnamon stick

1 dried chilli, cracked, seeds removed

2 red onions, peeled and cut into large wedges

2 red peppers cut into thick chunks

10 cloves of garlic

150ml water

40g fresh ginger, peeled and grated

juice of 1 orange

1 tbsp harissa or (for a less spicy result) tomato paste

100g pitted dates

Heat the oven to 200°C/180°C fan.

Peel and halve the pumpkin, scoop out the seeds and cut it into large chunks.

Mix with the quince, the olive oil and the salt and place in a large roasting tin in one layer. Add the cinnamon stick and the chilli and pop into the oven for 20 minutes.

Remove from the oven, add the red onion wedges, the red pepper and the whole garlic cloves and mix to coat. Return to the oven for 15 minutes. While it's roasting, mix together the water with ginger, orange juice, harissa (or tomato paste) and dates, stirring to combine.

Pour the liquid over the roasting tray, carefully flip the vegetables and fruit in the liquid and return to the oven for a final 20 minutes.

Remove, stir again carefully and serve with some cooked rice or cracked wheat.

▶▶

Zoe Adjonyoh
Yam and plantain peanut curry

The floury texture of boiled yam makes it akin to the famous Irish potato and it can be a great addition to curries and potages. This recipe combines my love of *nkatsenkwan* (groundnut stew) with the two simple Ghanaian staples of yam and plantain.

This was the way I ate it as a child, when the lamb had gone from the pot and there was always leftover peanut sauce (both my mum and dad cooked it in great vats), which you could then add to some boiled yam and plantain. It makes a great alternative veggie curry!

Vegan

300g puna yam

cooking salt

2–3 medium-ripe plantains

1 quantity peanut sauce, prepared up to the stage of adding the peanut butter and blending (see recipe overleaf)

For the chale sauce

400g can tomatoes or 250g fresh tomatoes

30g or 2 tbsp tomato purée

1 onion, roughly chopped

5cm fresh root ginger, grated (unpeeled if organic)

1 red scotch bonnet chilli, deseeded

1 tbsp dried chilli flakes

1 tsp sea salt

3 garlic cloves (optional)

►►

Have a bowl or pan of water ready before you start, as you'll need to put each peeled yam piece straight into water as you go to prevent them oxidizing and turning brown. Peel the yam and cut into slices, then rinse thoroughly in cold water to remove the starch.

Chop the yam, add to a large saucepan of lightly salted boiling water and cook for 10 minutes.

Meanwhile, peel the plantains and cut into chunks slightly larger than bite size. Add to the boiling yam at the 10-minute point and cook together for about a further 10 minutes until fork tender – they will continue to cook in the peanut sauce.

Strain, reserving the cooking water to use as vegetable stock for making the peanut sauce. Set the yam and plantain aside.

Place all the ingredients for the chale sauce in a blender and blend together until you have a fairly smooth paste.

For the peanut sauce

1 tbsp groundnut oil

1 onion, finely diced

1 tbsp extra-hot chilli powder

1 tbsp curry powder

1 garlic clove, crushed

5cm piece fresh root ginger,
grated (unpeeled if organic)

1 red scotch bonnet
chilli, pierced

3 tbsp crushed roasted peanuts

2 tsp sea salt

1 tsp freshly ground
black pepper

500ml good quality
vegetable stock

100–200g organic peanut
butter, depending on how thick
you want the sauce

To garnish

chopped red chillies

sliced spring onions
or puréed basil

Make the peanut sauce. Heat the groundnut oil in a heavy-based saucepan. Add the onion and sauté over a medium heat for 2 minutes. Stir in the chilli powder and curry powder, then add the garlic, ginger, scotch bonnet, crushed peanuts, sea salt and black pepper and stir well – lots of punchy aromas should be rising from the pot at this point.

Stir in the chale sauce and vegetable stock and bring to the boil, then reduce the heat and simmer for 15–20 minutes.

Add the peanut butter 1 tbsp at a time, while stirring, until it has all dissolved, then use a stick blender to blend all the ingredients to a smooth consistency.

Add the boiled yam and plantain to the sauce and leave to simmer for 20 minutes, stirring in a little water as necessary to prevent any sticking.

Serve in a bowl garnished with chopped red chillies and a touch of greenery such as sliced spring onions or puréed basil.

Bluebells in the Natural
Area at Kew

Rosie Sykes
Parsnip and coconut cake

I think parsnip and coconut have similar flavour notes and so complement each other rather well in this cake. It is delicious with the coconut icing, but, equally, it makes a great pudding served warm without the icing, but with some ice cream or sorbet instead. Coconut would be a great choice!

Makes one 20cm cake

For the cake

175g coconut oil (plus a little extra to grease the tin), warm enough to spread but not melted

200g unrefined caster sugar

100g soft light brown sugar

zest and juice of 1 lemon

3 large free range eggs, beaten, (the cake will work more successfully if they are at room temperature)

250g parsnip, peeled and coarsely grated

50g desiccated coconut

250g self-raising flour

1½ tsp baking powder

For the icing

150g coconut oil, warm enough to spread

150g icing sugar

approx. 1 tsp warm water mixed with 1 tbsp lemon juice

20g desiccated coconut

Preheat the oven to 160°C/140°C fan. Grease a 20cm cake tin and line the base with baking paper.

While the oven is warming up, spread the 20g desiccated coconut (for the icing) out on a baking tray and let it toast in the oven in the increasing heat. You want it to be light golden brown. Set aside to cool.

To make the cake, put the coconut oil in mixing bowl and beat (preferably with an electric mixer) until soft and light. Add the sugars and lemon zest and cream them together until fluffy.

Gradually add the eggs. If the mixture starts to look as though it is curdling, add a bit of flour. Once all the eggs are in, carefully fold in the parsnip and desiccated coconut and then the flour and baking powder. Finally, loosen with the lemon juice.

Turn the mixture into the cake tin and bake for about 35–45 minutes. It is ready when it springs back when pressed and an inserted knife comes out clean.

Place on a cooling rack and after 10 minutes turn the cake out of the tin and leave it to get completely cold.

Once the cake is cold, it can be iced. Beat the coconut oil in a mixer as above and gradually add the icing sugar, beating between each addition. Once smooth and thick, very slowly drizzle in the warm water and lemon juice mixture. Once completely added, beat for a couple more minutes then leave to sit for 10 minutes before spreading over the cake. Sprinkle the toasted coconut over the iced cake. Give the icing 30 minutes to set before eating.

Anna Jones
Squash and crispy kale pizza

This is a maverick pizza. It has a squash purée where the tomato sauce might usually be; and no cheese, but instead a topping of crispy kale, toasted nuts and tomatoes. If you find the idea of pizza without cheese a bridge too far, some soft goat's cheese crumbled over the top at the end wouldn't be a disaster.

Vegan

Makes 4

1 large butternut squash (about 1kg), peeled, deseeded and cut into roughly 2cm chunks

2 sprigs rosemary, leaves stripped

1 good pinch dried chilli flakes

sea salt and black pepper

extra virgin olive oil

4–6 tbsp vegetable stock

250g kale, leaves stripped

30g toasted nuts (pine nuts, chopped almonds, walnuts, hazelnuts all work)

200g sun-blushed tomatoes, cut into rough halves

For the pizza dough

325g strong bread flour

125g wholemeal spelt flour

10g sea salt

5g fast-action dried yeast

285ml warm water

40ml olive oil, plus extra for cooking

semolina or extra bread flour, for dusting

Heat the oven to 200°C/180°C fan. Make the pizza dough according to the recipe below, or use your own favourite dough recipe. Put the squash into a roasting tray, add the rosemary and chilli, then season, drizzle with olive oil and toss.

Roast for an hour, or until soft, golden and cooked through. Remove from the tray and carefully tip into a food processor. Blitz to a spreadable paste, adding a little veg stock to loosen to the consistency of tomato sauce, if need be.

While the squash is cooking, roughly tear the kale into one layer on a large tray (you may need two). Toss with a drizzle of olive oil and some salt and pepper, and roast for 10–15 minutes, until crisp. Meanwhile, roast the nuts on a tray for 5 minutes, or until golden, then set aside.

For each pizza, top with 5 tbsp of butternut squash purée (if it has thickened on resting, loosen with more stock), spreading evenly in one layer. Transfer to the oven using the method in the dough recipe below and bake for 8 minutes.

Once cooked, top with the kale and sun-blushed tomatoes, and sprinkle with toasted nuts.

Easy pizza dough

I've written this recipe in such a way that you can make the pizza base two ways: to be topped and baked immediately, or to be par-cooked and frozen, ready to use whenever you need.

I make this in a stand mixer: put all the ingredients into the bowl and put on the highest setting for 12 minutes. If you are doing this by hand, mix the wet ingredients into the dry in a bowl and, once combined, knead on a dusted surface for 15 minutes – you want a very soft and stretchy dough. Put the dough back into the mixing bowl, cover with a damp tea towel and leave in a warm place to rest for an hour.

Tip the dough onto a clean work surface and divide into four roughly 200g portions. Make a claw with your hand around a piece of dough and, keeping your hand in contact with the table, make small, circular motions to mould each one into a tight, round ball.

Put a good glug of olive oil in a large roasting tin and roll the dough balls around, coating them with oil; this will stop them sticking together. Leave covered with a damp tea towel in a warm place to rise for an hour or so.

Turn the oven to the maximum temperature, above 230°C/210°C fan. If you have a baking stone or thick baking sheet, put it in the oven to warm. Scatter a good amount of flour on to a work surface, then, using a rolling pin, roll out the bases as thinly as you can, rotating them as you go.

If you are eating them straight away, add your preferred toppings. If you are pre-baking them for later, cook them untopped. Carefully transfer each pizza or base to a cool, flat baking sheet dusted with flour to stop them from sticking, then shuffle on to the hot stone or baking sheet.

To par-bake the bases, cook one at a time for a couple of minutes, until they are lightly coloured. Once cool, stack with a small square of baking paper between each one and put in the freezer; they'll also keep in the fridge for a few days. To cook from frozen, top and bake for 5 minutes at your hottest oven temperature (over 230°C/210°C fan) for 8–10 minutes, until golden.

For a topped pizza, cook one at a time for 5–8 minutes, until golden.

Martin Allen Morales
Oca with cashew and chipotle sauce

Oca is an exquisite tuber I enjoyed eating as a kid growing up in Peru. It's native to the Andean region, grown 3,000m above sea level, and has been used in cooking for the last 1,000 years. I've tried to keep the essence of this vegetable so you can enjoy both the sweet and savoury nature in its truest form so here, I suggest poaching it. I've partnered it with a sauce I created inspired by the sauces of the city of Arequipa in Peru which is known as the heartland of traditional cooking. Here women chefs, entrepreneurial daughters and granddaughters of generations of Picanteras (women who run Picanterias – family-run traditional lunchtime eateries) have over the years shown me how to make the very best sauces and dishes. These are made using no electricity, no blenders nor mixers. Simply by hand with a grinding stone which is the size and shape of a neck travel pillow but weighing over 5kg! The process is slow but by combining the flavours in this way they texturize together more harmoniously and deliciously. However, you can use a blender if you want and one day, just make sure you visit Arequipa.

Serves 4

2 tsp salt

800g oca (alternately, use new potatoes, baby turnips or broccoli spears)

150g fresh peas

30g crushed cashew nuts, to garnish

finely chopped leaves of 1 stem of tarragon, to garnish

For the sauce

7 crushed garlic cloves

2 tbsp olive oil

3 tbsp chipotle paste

4 small stems each of coriander, mint and tarragon, leaves picked

400ml single cream

50g cashew nuts

50g grated Parmesan

2 digestive biscuits

salt and cayenne pepper to taste

Place 400ml of water in a pan and add in 2 tsp salt. Bring to the boil and add the oca and peas, stirring them into the salty water. Cover and gently poach these until soft. This should take just under 10 minutes. Set aside, drain and let the steam poach these further.

To make the sauce, place the crushed garlic cloves and olive oil in a pan and heat on a medium heat for 3–5 minutes, stirring until soft and slightly golden. Add the chipotle paste first, next the coriander, mint and tarragon leaves, and then the cream. Keep stirring for a minute to warm up the sauce, but do not let it boil. Take the sauce off the heat and blend it a blender, adding the cashews, Parmesan and finally the biscuits to thicken the dip. Season with salt and cayenne pepper.

Place the oca and peas in a serving bowl and drizzle the sauce over them. Sprinkle with crushed cashews and chopped tarragon to add a little texture and serve at once.

Oca grown in the Kew
kitchen garden

The Rock Garden and
Davies Alpine House

Ed Smith
Braised portobello mushrooms with
judion beans and chimichurri

Lara Lee
Asian mushroom and baby potato stir-fry

Thane Prince
Steamed mushroom pudding

Uyen Luu
Assorted mushrooms and Jerusalem artichoke
summer rolls

FUNGI

MiMi Aye
Shan-style chanterelle salad: *hmo thingan thoke*

Anja Dunk
Mushroom and walnut paté

Roopa Gulati
Mixed mushrooms with tomatoes and cumin

Rukmini Iyer
Red wine mushroom casserole with a cheese cobbler topping

Xanthe Clay
Roasted hispi cabbage with soy, mushrooms
and fennel fronds

The world of fungi is a fascinating one. Neither plant nor animal, fungi belong to their own separate biological kingdom, along with yeasts and moulds. Interestingly, fungi are more closely related to animals than to plants. Often disregarded, they play a vital role in the cycle of life, recycling nutrients in ecosystems back into the soil to help plants to grow. Unlike plants who source energy from the sun via photosynthesis, fungi release digestive enzymes into the environment that, for example, break down wood and other plant matter. Fungi are also central to our everyday life, with medicines such as penicillin and food and drink such as cheese, bread and beer all based on fungi.

Mushrooms are the reproductive structure and make up just a fraction of the total fungus. The main body of the fungus – formed of myriad fine threads called hyphae – is called the mycelium and it is usually hidden out of sight underneath soil or rotting wood. For centuries, wild mushrooms have been sought out and picked by people around the world to supplement their diet, albeit with careful attention as many mushrooms cause unpleasant side-effects when eaten, while some are toxic. The truffle, a fungal fruiting body noted for its strong, distinctive aroma, is particularly prized. Unlike most other mushrooms, truffles produce their fruiting bodies underground, so truffle hunters use specially trained dogs and pigs with keen noses to sniff out these valuable fungi in the forests where they grow. The region of Piedmont in Italy is noted for its white truffles and Perigord in France for its black truffles. A classic way of enjoying truffles in Italy is freshly shaved over a simple bowl of just-cooked pasta. In Japanese cuisine, with its emphasis on freshness and seasonality, the matsutake mushroom, which grows wild in Japan's pine forests in the autumn months, is a highly prized delicacy. In Europe, wild porcini, ceps or penny bun mushrooms are eagerly sought out. With their rich, almost meaty flavour, fresh porcini can be enjoyed in many ways – simply eaten raw, finely sliced, in salads, fried in olive oil, cooked in omelettes, risottos or pasta dishes.

The pleasures edible mushrooms offer include those of texture as well as flavour. One sees this aspect in Chinese cuisine, where mushrooms such as wood ear mushrooms (which are dried, soaked, then cooked before eating) are enjoyed for their particular springy crunchiness. Mushrooms are 80–90 per cent water, so when cooked – subjected to heat – they shrink quickly and noticeably. Drying mushrooms is not only an excellent way of preserving a very perishable ingredient, it also concentrates their flavour admirably. Dried shiitake mushrooms (also called simply 'Chinese mushrooms'), have a savoury depth of flavour and a distinctive chewy texture and are an important ingredient in Chinese cuisine. The most highly prized are called 'flower mushrooms'; these have thick, round caps with a distinctive cracked pattern. Dried shiitake are used in a variety of ways in Chinese cooking: their caps are filled with a mixture of minced pork and then steamed, they are used in braised dishes and soups, and in lotus-leaf wrapped glutinous rice parcels, a classic dim sum dish. Using dried porcini, sliced or in powder form, is an excellent way of giving an umami boost to dishes containing cultivated mushrooms, such as soups or stews.

Human beings have long cultivated mushrooms as a food source. In China, shiitake have been cultivated for around 1,000 years. In France, the cultivation of the common white mushroom began in the 17th century in quarry tunnels. The mushroom species which can be most successfully cultivated are decomposers, those which break down dead plant materials. Many other edible mushrooms, including the sought-after porcini, grow in a symbiotic relationship with trees in a forest. These species have proved harder to grow commercially. Mushroom kits (consisting of a substrate inoculated with mycelium) for would-be home growers are now readily available.

Kew has a long history of research into fungi. The Fungarium, founded in 1879, houses Kew's reference collection of fungi. Estimated at 1.25 million dried specimens, this collection is the largest in the world, and also one of the oldest and most scientifically important. It contains samples of fungi from all seven continents, spanning the entire fungal tree of life and representing well over half of known global diversity. Among the collection are samples collected by the naturalists Charles Darwin, Alexander von Humboldt and John Ray. The children's writer Beatrix Potter, who was a keen mycologist, visited the Fungarium to examine specimens there. Kew's fungal collections are particularly rich in type specimens: original material that is used to make unequivocal links between the fungus as a living organism and the name applied to it. Recent advances in DNA technologies mean that these types can be sequenced and included in phylogenetic research.

It is estimated that a mere 7 per cent of fungal species in the world have been scientifically discovered or described, leaving an extraordinary 93 per cent to explore. In 2014, Kew scientists bought a packet of dried Chinese porcini mushrooms in London. Using DNA sequence methods they discovered, much to their surprise, that this one packet contained three new, previously scientifically unnamed species of porcini. In Kew's State of the World's Plants and Fungi 2020 report, the potential offered by fungi to help tackle environmental issues was made clear. Within the bioenergy sector, for example, fungi can both enhance bioenergy recovery from plants and produce more energy from the waste products of bioenergy processes.

Fungi have long been used in traditional medicine in countries around the world and many ground-breaking new medicines were first discovered in fungi. Kew's work on understanding the distribution of drug-like compounds in the fungal kingdom has the potential to aid discovery of new medicines and help to elucidate the evolutionary processes that underpin their biosynthesis.

In the complex web of life, fungi and plants are closely interwoven. Ninety per cent of all known terrestrial plant species form symbiotic interactions via their roots with naturally occurring fungi in the soil, forming mycorrhizas (fungus roots). It is increasingly understood that in order for trees to thrive in stressful urban environments they need supporting mycorrhizal fungi. Looking forward, it is clear that exploring and understanding the vast world of fungi offers the possibility of helping humanity and the environment in many ways.

Fungi in the Natural
Area at Kew

Ed Smith
Braised portobello mushrooms with judion beans and chimichurri

One of my favourite things about portobello and other large, flat mushrooms, is how, when braised gently rather than speedily fried, they become rich, intense, almost meaty ... and also extremely juicy. Paired with pre-cooked beans, braised mushrooms make for a pretty much hands-free, one tin meal. Though to enliven things a little just before serving, I like adding a sharp burst of a piquant sauce, such as an Argentinian chimichurri.

On which note, you could make the chimichurri detailed here while waiting for the mushrooms and beans to do their thing in the oven. However, the secret ingredient in the best versions of this condiment is time – if you can leave the ingredients to mellow mingle for 24 hours or more, you will be rewarded. This serves four as a light lunch or starter, which could be bolstered with some warmed, crunchy bread and perhaps some peppery rocket or watercress nearby. Alternatively, treat it as a hearty meal for two, with leftovers for another day.

Serves 4

For the mushrooms and beans
50g salted butter
8 large portobello mushrooms
1 x 720g jar pre-cooked judion (butter) beans
7 sprigs oregano
salt and freshly ground black pepper
2 large cloves garlic, thinly sliced

For the chimichurri
3 cloves garlic, minced
5 tbsp finely chopped parsley leaves
2 tbsp finely chopped oregano leaves
1 tsp dried chilli flakes
2 tbsp red wine vinegar
5 tbsp extra virgin olive oil
2 tsp flaky salt dissolved into 150ml water

To make the chimichurri, chop and measure the garlic, herbs, chilli, vinegar and oil into a Tupperware or sealable jar. Mix well, add the salt water, mix some more and then cover, refrigerate and leave to mellow and mingle in the fridge for at least a day. You will have leftovers – which if refrigerated will last for up to 3 weeks.

For the mushrooms and beans, you will need either a large hob and oven proof sauté pan or skillet into which the mushrooms fit in one layer. Or a frying pan, plus a roasting tin into which the mushrooms fit snuggly.

Heat the oven to 170°C/150°C fan.

Melt half the butter in a large ovenproof skillet or frying pan until foaming. Add the mushrooms, curved side down and cook without turning for 2–3 minutes until browned. Remove from the heat and transfer the mushrooms, momentarily, to a plate.

If your pan is not ovenproof, now is the time to grab your roasting tin.

Decant the beans and their juices into the skillet or roasting tin. Add another 300ml–400ml water, so that the beans are just submerged. Mix six of the oregano sprigs into the beans, then arrange the mushrooms in the cooking dish, pushing them down a little so that some of the liquid comes up their sides and they're not just sitting on top.

To serve

1–2 tbsp chimichurri per person

extra virgin olive oil

warmed, crusty bread

Season the inside of each mushroom generously with salt and pepper, add the sliced garlic and leaves picked from one sprig of oregano. Dot the remaining butter inside the mushrooms too.

Take a piece of greaseproof paper, wet it, screw it up then unravel it and place it over the mushrooms, tucking it in at the edge. Bake for 25 minutes, then remove the paper, baste the mushrooms with a little broth and bake for 5 minutes more. The mushrooms will have shrunken and might look dry, but should be juicy when you cut into them.

Transfer the beans and broth into four bowls, add two mushrooms per person, and 1–2 tbsp of chimichurri onto each portion. Finish with a good glug of extra virgin olive oil and serve – with warmed crusty bread and peppery leaves nearby if you wish.

Lara Lee

Asian mushroom and baby potato stir-fry

Mushrooms and potatoes are the heroes of this vegan stir-fry. A sauce of Shaoxing wine, tamarind and soy is soaked up by these porous vegetables, amplifying their earthy flavours to the max. The mix of Asian mushrooms sing brightly in this dish, alongside crispy, golden discs of pan-fried potatoes, crunchy mangetout and cashews and the citrusy freshness of coriander leaves. Serve with steamed rice.

Vegan

Serves 2

neutral oil, such as sunflower or rapeseed

380g Asian mushrooms, such as king oyster thinly sliced, oyster mushrooms whole or torn into chunks, and shiitakes thickly sliced

200g baby potatoes, thinly sliced

50g cashews

60g mangetout, trimmed

sea salt

2 tbsp soy sauce

2 tbsp Shaoxing rice wine

2 tsp tamarind paste

small handful coriander leaves (about 5g)

Heat 1 tbsp of oil in a non-stick large wok or frying pan on a high heat and cook half of the mushrooms for 3 minutes until golden. Heat another tbsp of oil in the pan and repeat with the remaining mushrooms. Set aside.

Wipe out the pan and heat 2 tbsp of oil on high. Add the potatoes and cook for 10 minutes, stirring every so often, until they are cooked through and beginning to colour. Set aside and wipe out the pan.

Heat ½ tbsp of oil in the pan and add the cashews for 30 seconds, then add the mangetout with a large pinch of salt and a splash of water and cook for a further 2 minutes until cooked through.

Return the mushrooms and potato to the pan and add the soy sauce, Shaoxing wine and tamarind, stirring everything together until the ingredients are warmed through and the sauce has evaporated.

Stir through the coriander leaves just before serving (reserving a little for garnish) and serve immediately.

Thane Prince
Steamed mushroom pudding

Mushroom soy is wonderfully full of flavour and very dark in colour. It can be bought from Oriental food shops, but if it is not available use a good quality Japanese soy for this pudding.

Serves 4

450g very fresh mushrooms
(chestnut mushrooms are good)

2 tbsp olive oil

1 large onion peeled
and chopped

4 sticks celery, chopped

1 plump clove garlic,
peeled and chopped

1 tbsp butter

1 heaped tbsp flour

300ml vegetable stock

2 tbsp medium sherry

2 tbsp mushroom soy sauce

½ tsp tarragon leaves

black pepper

Suet pastry

225g plain flour

a good pinch of salt

1½ tsp baking powder

110g vegetable suet

approx. 150–175ml cold water

Wipe the mushrooms, trimming the stems and cut large ones in half.

In a large frying pan heat the oil then fry the onion and celery until they begin to colour. Add the garlic and butter and continue to cook for 2–3 minutes. Now add the mushrooms and stir well. Cook for a further 2–3 minutes. Sprinkle on the flour, stir until it has absorbed the oil then pour in the stock, soy and sherry. Season with pepper and simmer, stirring often until the sauce is thick.

Make the pastry: place the flour, salt, baking powder and suet in a bowl, add the water and mix until you have a dough. Knead for a moment or two then roll to give a 30cm circle. Cut one quarter from the circle and place to one side.

Grease a 900ml pudding bowl. Take up the larger piece of dough and use this to line the bowl bringing the cut edges together and pressing to seal the seam. Spoon in the filling and use the reserved dough, re rolled, to make a top. Press the edges to seal. Cover with a double sheet of buttered, pleated greaseproof paper, tying this on with string.

Place the bowl in a steamer or a large saucepan, fill half way with boiling water and steam for 1½ hours, checking the water level from time to time.

When cooked, uncover and run a palette knife carefully around the edge of the pudding. Invert onto a hot plate and serve at once with a green vegetable such as Savoy cabbage or baby kale.

Uyen Luu

Assorted mushrooms and Jerusalem artichoke summer rolls

The combination of fungi with a root vegetable and various perfumed leaves make eating these rolls a full-on sensory experience. Load with a variety of mushrooms and as many Vietnamese herbs as you can get hold of.

These exquisite rolls are packed with contrasting flavours and textures. The cooked mushrooms are soft, silky, meaty and smooth – they balance and marry with the crunchy Jerusalem artichoke. The refreshing raw herbs and rice noodles are their opposites, but together they complement each other. Dipped together with the sweet, sour, umami and hot sauce with the crunch of nuts sprinkled on top, these are beautiful and delicious. Raw and cooked, soft and crunchy, sweet and sour, hot and fresh, earthy and zesty. Yin and Yang.

Makes 6

For the mushrooms

10g butter

1 tsp olive oil

1 small round shallot, sliced

2 cloves of garlic, finely chopped

150g assorted mushrooms, sliced

1 tbsp oyster sauce or mushroom sauce

pinch of black pepper

For the Jerusalem artichoke

10g butter

60g Jerusalem artichoke, sliced into matchsticks

For the salad

12 coriander sprigs, stems and leaves roughly chopped

18 mint leaves, roughly chopped

18 cockscombe mint leaves (optional)

18 perilla leaves (optional)

12 fish mint leaves (optional)

12 Vietnamese coriander leaves (optional)

6 garlic chives (optional)

In a hot frying pan, on medium high heat, add the butter and a drop of olive oil and the shallot. Once it starts to colour add the garlic and watch until they both start to turn golden. Add the sliced mushrooms to the pan with the oyster or mushroom sauce and a good pinch of black pepper. Stir-fry for a few minutes until the mushrooms are soft and wilted. Set aside in a bowl to cool. Using the same frying pan on medium high heat, add a little butter and throw in the Jerusalem artichoke matchsticks. Let sit for a minute then toss and stir them for 2 minutes, achieving charred sides. Set aside in another bowl to cool.

Wash and spin or air dry the salad leaves (to keep the rice paper from breaking later on) and set aside. Rehydrate the rice vermicelli. Drain in a colander, rinse the starch off with hot water and cover with a lid for about 15 minutes to fluff up.

Pour some cold tap water into a tray deep and large enough to dip the rice paper into. Dip the rice paper sheet in for 1 second to moisten it, then place onto a chopping board.

If you think of the round paper as a face, at the bottom centre of the paper, where the mouth would be, line up the mushrooms and a line of artichoke, then the herbs, noodles and lettuce. Fold the two sides in (where the ears would be) then fold over the bottom flap (the chin) up to cover the ingredients. It should look like you are making an envelope. Then, as tightly as possible, starting from the bottom, roll and push down as you go along until you have reached the end of the rice paper. Repeat the process with the remaining rice paper sheets.

80g vermicelli noodles, rehydrate with boiling water from the kettle until soft and cooked

6 leaves of soft lettuce or Cos lettuce

For the hoisin and peanut butter dipping sauce

1 tsp vegetable oil

1 garlic clove, finely chopped

1 bird eye chilli, finely chopped

2 tbsp hoisin sauce

1/2 tbsp white wine vinegar or cider vinegar

1 tsp caster sugar

1 tbsp water

1 heaped tbsp smooth or crunchy peanut butter (optional)

2 tbsp peanuts, cashew or pistachio, crushed or blended (optional)

6 x 22cm rice paper sheets

Keep the rolls in an airtight container at room temperature and serve within 2–3 hours.

To make the dipping sauce, heat the oil in a saucepan. Fry the garlic until it browns slightly then add the chilli, hoisin sauce, vinegar, sugar, water and peanut butter. Combine together and bring to a gentle boil.

Pour the sauce into dipping bowls and sprinkle crushed nuts on top. Serve with the summer rolls.

The Rock Garden

MiMi Aye

Shan-style chanterelle salad:
hmo thingan thoke

Chanterelles grow sporadically throughout the Shan State in Burma, where the weather is cool, and in the mining town of Mogok which is right on the Shan State border and where my mother is from. These wild mushrooms appear after the monsoon rains around September time and are known in Burmese as *hmo thingan* because of how much they are revered and because of their golden hue – *hmo* means mushroom and *thingan* are the saffron robes of a Buddhist monk (*thoke* just means salad).

Because of their rarity as well as their fine flavour, chanterelles are expensive there and considered a real gem – the irony being that Mogok is renowned for its rubies. The mushrooms are sold at markets wrapped up in the leaves of the *Dipterocarpus tuberculatus* (known as *inn* in Burmese) because they are often found near these trees. These verdant parcels are kept fastened with wooden toothpicks, but the foragers are always delighted to display the treasures inside. In Mogok, chanterelles tend to be turned into this Shan-style salad which is served along with rice, some kind of curry, and a simple soup.

Vegan

Serves 2 or 1 hungry person as a side or starter

For the crispy noodles

20g dried egg/wheat noodles (about ½ a standard nest)

vegetable oil for frying

For the salad

½ banana shallot, sliced lengthways

150–200g chanterelle mushrooms

juice of ¼ lemon

⅛ tsp (small pinch) salt

⅛ tsp (small pinch) MSG

Snap the dried noodles into half and then boil them in a saucepan with plenty of water until al dente. Drain the cooked noodles and pat them as dry as possible with kitchen paper.

Thoroughly dry the saucepan as well and then heat 5cm depth of oil on a high heat in the same pan. When you can feel waves of heat above the pan with the palm of your hand, gently drop the cooked noodles into the hot oil. They should crisp up and brown almost immediately. Drain the crispy noodles on some kitchen paper, but reserve the oil. Set both to one side.

Slice the shallot as thinly as possible (a mandoline is best) and leave to soak in a bowl of cold water to take away any astringency and to firm the slices up.

Clean the mushrooms and then slice them into strips with a sharp knife. Heat 1 tbsp of the reserved oil on a high heat in a frying pan. When the oil is hot, add the mushroom strips and sauté for 1 minute. Turn off heat and leave the sautéed mushrooms to wilt on the hob.

Drain the sliced shallots and pat them dry with kitchen paper.

Place the sliced shallots and the sautéed mushrooms in a serving dish or shallow bowl. Add the lemon juice, salt and MSG. Gently toss everything together and crumble the crispy noodles on top.

Serve the salad while the mushrooms are still warm.

Cook's notes

You may have too many crispy noodles, but they make an excellent snack. You should also use the rest of the reserved oil to dress other salads, noodle dishes, rice dishes and more. In Burmese, we call this condiment *si chet* – cooked oil.

Anja Dunk
Mushroom and walnut paté

Brown food is having a bit of a renaissance at the moment and mushroom paté is a perfect example of why – it isn't the prettiest of things to spread on toast, but don't let that fool you into believing it isn't one of the best. Walnuts add a creamy, nutty flavour to the 'meaty' mushrooms. It's perfect Sunday night fare, spread on hot buttered toast, but equally as good in a sandwich or wrap for lunch. Stored wrapped up, paté keeps well in the fridge for up to 5 days.

Vegan

Serves 4

3 tbsp rapeseed oil

1 small white onion, peeled and finely diced

250g mushrooms, sliced (field, brown, button – all work)

2 garlic cloves, peeled and sliced

1 tbsp fresh thyme leaves (or lemon thyme)

50g walnut pieces

juice of ½ lemon

salt and freshly ground black pepper

Heat the oil in a frying pan over a high heat. Once hot, add the onion and mushrooms and fry for around 6 minutes, stirring occasionally to avoid burning. Now add the garlic, thyme and walnut pieces and cook for a further 4 minutes, stirring from time to time until the onions start to turn golden and the walnuts toast slightly around the edges.

Tip the contents of the frying pan into a food processor, add the lemon juice and seasoning. Blitz for a minute or two until the desired consistency is reached.

Spoon the paté into a dish and serve spread on hot toast or crackers.

Roopa Gulati
Mixed mushrooms with tomatoes and cumin

This simple recipe is popular across North India – buttery mushrooms are folded into a golden-fried onion and tomato masala seasoned with warming garam masala, astringent turmeric and toasted cumin.

Serves 4–6

4 tomatoes

4 tbsp sunflower oil

1 tsp cumin seeds

1 onion, finely sliced

4 garlic cloves, finely chopped

20g root ginger, peeled
and finely chopped

¼ tsp turmeric

½ tsp Kashmiri chilli powder

½ tsp garam masala

1 tsp caster sugar

2 tbsp single cream

50g unsalted butter

300g chestnut mushrooms,
quartered

150g oyster mushrooms

2 tbsp chopped coriander

boiled rice or Indian bread,
to serve

Bring a pan of water to the boil. Turn off the heat and submerge the tomatoes in the water for about 30 seconds and then remove the skin with a sharp knife and roughly chop the flesh. Leave on one side.

Heat the oil in a wok or karahi over a medium-high heat. Add the cumin and fry, stirring all the time, for about 30 seconds, until the seeds release a nutty aroma.

Stir in the sliced onion and fry for 7–10 minutes until golden. Turn the heat to medium, add the garlic and ginger, and continue cooking for 1–2 minutes.

Add the turmeric, chilli powder and garam masala, followed by the chopped tomatoes and sugar. Cook the masala without a lid for 7–10 minutes until the tomatoes have softened and thickened.

Pour in 150ml of hot water and add the cream and simmer the sauce for another 2–3 minutes until it has a coating consistency – add a little more water if needed. Cover the pan and leave on one side.

Heat the butter in a frying pan over a medium-high heat and cook the chestnut mushrooms until browned. Stir in the oyster mushrooms for the last minute of cooking and then add them to the tomato masala. Bring everything to a simmer and stir in the chopped coriander before serving with boiled rice or Indian bread.

Rukmini Iyer

Red wine mushroom casserole with a cheese cobbler topping

This casserole is incredibly warming for a cold autumn night – rich with wine and mushrooms and with herby cheese scones as a topping. You can easily double this up to serve more people – just use a really large roasting tin.

Serves 2

300g mini portobello mushrooms

250g chestnut mushrooms, halved

3 cloves of garlic, crushed

2 tsp sea salt

1 onion, roughly chopped

2–3 sprigs of fresh rosemary

1 tbsp olive oil

200ml good red wine

2 tsp cornflour

150ml vegetable stock

For the scones

250g plain flour

1½ tsp cream of tartar

1 tsp sea salt

35g cold butter, cubed

25g fresh parsley or basil, finely chopped

60g extra mature Cheddar, grated

freshly ground black pepper

100ml milk

1 egg, lightly beaten

Preheat the oven to 200°C/180°C fan. Mix the mushrooms, garlic, sea salt, onion and rosemary with the olive oil in a roasting tin or lasagne dish, then transfer to the oven and roast for 20 minutes.

Meanwhile, in a food processor or by hand, mix the flour, cream of tartar and sea salt with the butter until it looks like fine sand, then stir in the herbs, three quarters of the cheese and the pepper. Add the milk and bring everything together gently into a scone dough. Cover and chill until needed.

Once the mushrooms have had their 20 minutes, mix a tablespoon of the red wine with the cornflour, then stir it into the mushrooms along with the remaining wine and the stock.

Form the scone dough into walnut-size portions and dot them over the mushrooms, flattening each slightly. Brush with the beaten egg, top with the reserved cheese, then return to the oven for 20 minutes – the scones should be golden brown and crisp, and the sauce thick and reduced. Leave to sit for 5 minutes, then serve hot.

Xanthe Clay
Roasted hispi cabbage with soy, mushrooms and fennel fronds

A simple one pan supper, using whatever mushrooms you can get your hands on. Shoyu or tamari makes it super savoury – both are just Japanese soy sauce, but they have a lighter flavour than Chinese versions. Kikkoman is the most famous brand of shoyu but Clearspring make a good version too, as well as the wheat-free, gluten free tamari. More Japanese sprinkles go over the top: shichimi togarashi is a chilli and spice mix which includes sesame, but it's fine to use simple sesame and chilli too.

Vegan

**Serves 2 hungry people
or 4 with other dishes**

1 hispi cabbage weighing around 1kg

300g mixed mushrooms

1 tbsp sesame oil (or olive oil)

4 tbsp tamari or shoyu

250g cooked beluga lentils (or other firm lentils, not the kind that collapse when cooked)

a generous handful of fennel fronds (the flowers too, if they are out)

1 tbsp of togarashi shichimi or toasted sesame seeds mixed with a pinch of chilli flakes

150ml Greek yoghurt or dairy-free yoghurt

Preheat the oven as high as it will go – 250°C/230°C fan ideally.

Cut the cabbage into 8 wedges, through the root. Slice the mushrooms 1cm thick or tear them into chunks. Brush a large shallow baking tray with oil and lay the cabbage on top. Scatter over the mushrooms. Brush with the rest of the oil and splash over the tamari or shoyu sauce.

Bake the veg for about 15 minutes, until the edges of the cabbage are turning dark brown. Keep an eye on them as they may take less or more time, depending on your oven. Turn the cabbage slices, pressing them into any juices that have accumulated in the pan, and bake for another 15 minutes until browned on the other side. They should look verging on burnt.

Scatter over the lentils and return to the oven for 5 minutes to warm through. Meanwhile, chop the fennel fronds.

Remove the tray from the oven, and scatter over the togarashi shichimi, or sesame and chilli, then the fennel fronds. Dot with spoonfuls of yoghurt and serve.

The Agius Evolution Garden
and Temple of Aeolus

Meera Sodha
Burmese mango salad with peanut and lime

Christine McFadden
Roasted peppered pear salad with
sheep's cheese, honey and walnuts

Hattie Ellis
Romesco sauce

Florence Knight
Barley ice cream with honey-roasted grapes

Sybil Kapoor
Japanese sweet potato fritters
and banana ice cream

 # FRUITS AND NUTS

Sue Quinn
Cocoa hazelnut traybake with espresso Swiss meringue

Claudia Roden
Dried fruit compote with custard:
zurracapote con crema pastelera vasca

Chantelle Nicholson
Foraged blackberry and fig leaf upside-down pudding

Pam Corbin
Rosaceae jelly

Signe Johansen
Almond and hazelnut torte
with roasted plums and blackberries

Claire Ptak
Orange, ginger and rye upside-down cake

There is something very alluring about fruits – think of luscious, orange-fleshed mangoes, bright red strawberries, purple grapes, green and dark purple figs, pink-tinged peaches... their colours, their soft, appealing textures, their sweetness, their fragrance are all very inviting. This is deliberately so on the plant's part. Fruits contain seeds which the plants want to disperse, so they set out to attract animals to eat their ripe fruit in order to spread their seeds, beginning the plant life cycle anew. Nuts also contain seeds, but, in contrast to fruits, these edible seeds are contained within hard shells. Rich in nutrients, nuts have been valued as a food source since prehistoric times. Many nuts, such as brazil nuts, macadamias and pecans, are high in fat, which makes them a good source of energy.

In the days before refrigerators and freezers, there were a number of ways of preserving perishable fruit. Drying fruit such as grapes (which are then called raisins), plums (prunes), figs, apricots or apples was one simple and effective way. The Middle East has a long history of cooking fruits, such as apricot, into a purée, then spreading thin layers of the fruit purée to dry out in the sun to form fruit leather. Using sugar to conserve fruits by turning them into jams, marmalades, chutneys or fruit cheeses such as membrillo (quince paste) was also popular, especially as sugar became more affordable. The time-consuming process of candying fruit by dipping them repeatedly into a sugar syrup to create glace fruit has been used for centuries to create a luxurious treat. There is somehow a celebratory aspect to fruit. Understandably, given their natural sweetness, they are a key component of desserts around the world: Thailand's mango with coconut rice, France's tarte au citron, America's apple pie, England's strawberries and cream. That balance of acidity and sweetness which fruits such as apples, apricots or oranges possess means that they also work well in savoury dishes, making them hugely versatile.

Nuts continue to be a valued food to this day, enjoyed for their flavour and texture. Their use in the kitchen extends far beyond simply being a snack to enjoy with a drink. They are used in salads, cakes and pastries and to make rissoles and nut butters. Finely ground nuts are often used to thicken sauces in dishes such as India's korma or Indonesia's rendang. In Italy, pine nuts, the small, laboriously gathered seeds of the stone pine, are used in savoury dishes or ground to make pesto – and are also used in Tuscany's classic dessert torta della nonna. Pecan nuts, which are native to the southern states of the United States and the northern states of Mexico, are famously paired with another tree-based delicacy, maple syrup, to make pecan pie. In Indonesia, Malaysia and Singapore, a nut called *buah keluak* is a highly prized delicacy. Poisonous if eaten raw due to the fact the nuts contain hydrocyanic acid, they are cured in a time-consuming process that involves boiling, covering with ash, fermenting and soaking to make them edible, before they can be cooked in special celebratory dishes. The high fat content of certain nuts means that they can also be used to make oil, such as France's walnut oil, which is classically used for salad dressings.

The banana has a special place in Kew Gardens' history. Joseph Dalton Hooker, Kew's director from 1865 to 1885 used to send his good friend Charles Darwin bananas grown in the glasshouses at Kew. In a letter thanking Hooker, Darwin wrote 'you have not only rejoiced my soul, but my stomach, for the bananas are simply delicious. I never saw any like them'. Today, the banana is the world's most popular fruit and we take its ready availability for granted. In fact, it is in a precarious state. In the 1950s, Panama disease, caused by a fungus, almost wiped out the Gros Michel banana cultivar. A new strain of the same disease threatens the Cavendish banana that we eat today. Grown by cloning, the Cavendish is vulnerable to pathogens as it cannot adapt to fight them. The Crop Wild Relatives Project, in which Kew have worked alongside the Crop Trust, seeks to preserve biodiversity and crop resilience by gathering and conserving seeds of wild relatives of key crops. Wild bananas, threatened by deforestation and urbanisation, are disappearing quickly. As part of the project's work, samples of nine different wild bananas have been collected in Kenya, Nepal and Vietnam and stored as a useful genetic resource for banana breeders.

Spanning Europe and Asia, the Caucasus represents one of the most diverse and endangered biodiversity hotpots in the world, with around 6,400 known plant species, of which more than 25 per cent are endemic. The region also harbours a remarkable concentration of economically important plants, with around 2,000 species having a direct economic value and used for timber, food, medicines and dyes. Of these, over 15 per cent are wild-growing fruits, including wild berries and nuts. Major contemporary threats to wild fruit and nut populations include illegal logging, fuel-wood harvesting, overgrazing and pollution.

Some of these important wild fruit and nut populations survived the Ice Age; their protection would provide the scientific community with access to unique traits of resistance and tolerance, as well as ensuring the reliant, rural communities who harvest these wild species have continued income, medical resources and diverse diets. Kew is working closely with collaborators in Georgia and Armenia to ensure the conservation of wild fruit and nut species through collecting and safeguarding seeds of over 120 such species. Close engagement with local communities will be key to understanding their use of wild fruits and nuts, and will help support sustainable wild harvesting into the future.

We take the abundance of fruits and nuts we enjoy for granted, but the pressures facing plants and endangering their survival are real. Seeking to research and conserve them as Kew does has never been more vital.

Meera Sodha
Burmese mango salad with peanut and lime

This is inspired by a dish I ate at one of my favourite restaurants in Mumbai called Burma Burma, so it is that I offer up my memory of its mighty and mouth-watering mango, peanut and lime salad. When freshly made, this salad is great by itself or with seasoned and fried tofu, but if left a day it will release delicious juices and is wonderful with rice noodles. Make sure you buy the hardest, greenest, most unripe mangoes you can find, because ripe mangoes will juice when you cut them.

Vegan

Serves 4

2cm fresh ginger, peeled and julienned

1 bird's-eye chilli, finely chopped

5 tbsp lime juice (from 3 limes)

1 tsp salt

rapeseed oil

1 onion, halved and thinly sliced

4 cloves of garlic, thinly sliced

1½ tbsp chickpea flour

2 tbsp crunchy peanut butter

½ a sweetheart cabbage, finely shredded

2 unripe mangoes (500g)

2 medium carrots (200g), peeled and julienned

a handful of fresh mint leaves

a handful of fresh coriander leaves

a large handful (60g) of crushed salted peanuts

Put the ginger and chilli into a bowl, add the lime juice and salt, and leave to steep.

Put a plate by the stove and cover it with a piece of kitchen paper. Heat 5 tbsp of oil in a non-stick frying pan over a medium flame and, when smoking hot, add the onion. Separate the slices using a wooden spoon and fry, stirring once or twice, until brown and crisp. Scoop out with a slotted spoon and put on the prepared plate. Fry the garlic in the same pan for 2 minutes, until golden brown (be watchful: it cooks quickly), then transfer to the plate.

Stir the chickpea flour into the remaining hot oil in the pan over a very low heat to create a paste. Stir constantly for a minute, then add the peanut butter, stir for another minute and take off the heat.

Put the cabbage into a large bowl. Peel the mangoes and shave with a julienne peeler until you hit the stone; or, if cutting by hand, cut the cheeks from the stone on all four sides and julienne. Add the mango and carrots to the cabbage. Reserve a handful of the fried onion to garnish, then add the rest, together with the fried garlic, to the cabbage. Toss, then pour over the chickpea and peanut paste and the ginger, chilli and lime mixture, and toss again. Taste, and adjust the lime and salt if need be.

To serve, transfer the salad to a plate, add the herbs, toss one final time, and top with the crushed peanuts and remaining fried onions.

Christine McFadden
Roasted peppered pear salad with sheep's cheese, honey and walnuts

This is a simple but impressive starter that relies on top-quality ingredients. Peppercorns are particularly important – unnamed varieties will add little to the dish whereas Wynad or Tellicherry from Kerala, southwest India, are the Rolls Royce of peppercorns. Both have complex rich flavours and warm but not biting heat. You'll find them on-line and in good supermarkets.

Serves 4

2 large pears, dense-fleshed such as Conference or Fiorelle

½ level tsp sea salt flakes, plus extra for sprinkling

½ level tsp black peppercorns such as Wynad or Tellicherry

2 tsp mild clear honey such as acacia or orange blossom, plus extra for sprinkling

1 tsp extra virgin olive oil, plus extra for sprinkling

juice of ¼ lemon

6 tbsp water

4 small handfuls baby chard leaves or beet leaves

100g hard sheep cheese such as Lord of the Hundreds, Herriot Farmhouse or Swaledale, thinly sliced

8 shelled walnuts, new season 'wet' if possible, halved

aged balsamic vinegar or pomegranate molasses

Preheat the oven to 200°C/180°C. Slice the pears in half lengthways and remove the cores, interior stem and peel (see Cook's notes below). Place cut side up in a small roasting tin.

Combine the sea salt flakes and peppercorns, and lightly crush using a pestle and mortar. Sprinkle the mixture into the cavities of the pears, then spoon the honey over the top. Sprinkle with the olive oil and lemon juice. Pour the water into the base of the roasting tin.

Roast for 20–30 minutes, turning the tin halfway through, until the pears are beginning to brown at the edges. Carefully move them to a plate, pour over the juices from the roasting tin and leave to cool slightly.

Divide the chard or beet leaves between four serving plates. Place a warm pear half on top with a few slices of sheep's cheese to one side. Scatter the walnut halves over the pears and leaves. Sprinkle with more honey, a few drops of extra virgin olive oil, some crumbled sea salt flakes and a dribble of sticky aged balsamic vinegar.

Cook's notes

You need good quality peppercorns for this, preferably organic. Don't be tempted to use pre-ground pepper.

If you have one, use a melon baller to neatly scoop out the pear core.

The interior stem of the pear is the fibrous part that runs from the core to the exterior stem. Make a shallow V-shaped cut along its length then use the tip of your knife to remove it.

When preparing the pears, you'll find them easier to handle if you remove the peel after you've dealt with halving, coring etc.

Hattie Ellis
Romesco sauce

This colourful and delicious garlicy Catalan sauce, lightly thickened with almonds and breadcrumbs, is great with grilled vegetables and sauté potatoes, seafood, and meats such as lamb, chicken and sausages, brightening up a bbq and bringing southern sunshine flavours to any table.

Nutritious nuts are an excellent part of a plant-centred diet, providing protein, healthy fats and micronutrients and good to use in dishes and not only eaten as snacks. The sauce traditionally uses toasted almonds but you can use a convenient shortcut of almond butter instead. If you need to toast the almonds, put on a tray in a 180°C/160° fan oven for 8–10 minutes and cool slightly before using.

Vegan
Makes 8–12 servings

2 cloves garlic, finely grated or chopped

2 ready-roasted red pepper, roughly chopped – piquillo peppers best of all

2 large or 3 medium tomatoes (as red and ripe as possible), roughly chopped

1 fresh red chilli, seeded and chopped

1 tsp smoked paprika

flaky sea salt

4 tbsp almond butter or 50g toasted whole almonds

3 tbsp dried or fresh breadcrumbs, fried in 1 tbsp oil

25ml red wine vinegar

150ml olive oil

Put the garlic, peppers, tomatoes, chilli, smoked paprika and 1 tsp flaky sea salt in a food processor (plus the whole almonds, if using instead of almond butter). Pulse to a rough paste. Add the fried breadcrumbs and almond butter and pulse again.

Add the vinegar and, with the food processor running, pour the olive oil in a thin steam into the bowl of the food processor so it emulsifies into the sauce.

Taste the sauce, adding more salt, vinegar, and almond butter or ground-up almonds, if needed. The sauce keeps for a week or so in the fridge, covered.

Florence Knight
Barley ice cream with honey-roasted grapes

Barley is more popularly used in stews and soups, however during a trip to New York I came across a cornflake ice cream at a restaurant called Momofuku, and that inspired this recipe. The ice cream has a wonderful rice-y, wholesome taste, which works perfectly with the sticky, honeyed grapes.

Serves 4

300g pearl barley
125ml milk
750ml double cream
1 tbsp malt extract
10 medium egg yolks
175g caster sugar

For the grapes

1 large bunch seedless red grapes
1 tsp extra virgin olive oil
2 tbsp runny honey
4 sprigs of thyme
a pinch of salt

Preheat the oven to 180ºC/160ºC fan. Toast the barley on a tray for 5 minutes in the oven and set aside.

In a heavy bottomed pan, warm the milk, cream, barley and malt extract over a medium heat to just below boiling point.

Whisk the yolks and sugar in a large bowl until pale, fluffy and thick enough to hold a ribbon on the surface of the froth. Pour the hot milk and cream little by little over the fluffy yolks, stirring non-stop. Return the mixture to the pan and simmer gently, stirring constantly to stop the custard turning into scrambled egg.

When the custard is thick enough to coat the back of a spoon – I run my finger along the back to see that a line stays – it is ready. Remove from the heat, pour into a container and cover it with the cling film directly on the surface so that it doesn't form a skin. Chill in the fridge for 2 hours to infuse.

Strain the custard through a fine sieve, pounding with a ladle to squeeze out as much of that barley flavour as possible. Discarding the gloopy barley, pour the strained custard into an ice cream machine and churn until frozen. Alternatively, pour the mixture into a shallow tray and freeze for 30 minutes. Take it out and whisk through before returning to the freezer. Whisk and refreeze three or four times until smooth and set.

Preheat the oven to 200ºC/180ºC fan. Pull the grapes off their stalks, rinse them under cold running water, and pierce them a few times with the tip of a knife. Place the grapes on a baking tray, drizzle over the olive oil and honey, sprinkle over the picked thyme leaves and salt and give the tray a shake to combine. Pop in the oven for 15–20 minutes until the grapes blister and caramelise. Scoop a ball of the ice cream and place on the warm grapes to serve.

Sybil Kapoor
Japanese sweet potato fritters and banana ice cream

Wander past the vibrant market stalls in Kochi's famous Sunday farmers' market in Shikoku, and you will come across a queue of people buying a mid-morning snack of sweet potato fritters. The region is famous throughout Japan for its ultra-sweet, golden-fleshed sweet potatoes. Their dry mealy chestnut-like texture turns to fluff in the fritter and is the perfect way to tempt those who dislike the dry, floury texture of some vegetables, such as squash and sweet potato.

Serves 4

For the fritters

500g large sweet potatoes, peeled and cut into 2–3cm pieces

corn oil, for frying

175g plain white flour, sifted

1 tsp baking powder

100g caster sugar

2 tsp fine sea salt

1 medium egg, beaten

For the banana ice cream

300ml double cream

1 vanilla pod

3 medium bananas

juice of 1 lemon

3 tbsp rum

140g caster sugar

4 egg yolks

Place the sweet potato chunks in a large bowl of cold water and leave to soak for 30 minutes.

Heat the oil in a deep-fat fryer to 180°C.

Drain the sweet potatoes and pat dry.

In a large bowl, mix together the flour, baking powder, sugar and salt. Make a well in the centre of the flour and gradually stir in the egg and 150ml water until it forms a smooth, thick batter.

Mix the sweet potato chunks into the batter.

Drop a few of the batter-coated sweet potatoes into the oil and fry for 6 minutes, until fluffy and golden brown. You don't want the temperature of the oil to drop below 180°C. Remove to paper towels and leave to cool while you continue to fry the remaining sweet potato chunks in small batches. Leave for a couple of hours or until cold.

Shortly before serving, reheat the oil to 180°C. Fry the fritters in batches until golden and crisp. Drain on paper towels and serve hot or warm. The second frying ensures that the fritters are crisp and fluffy when eaten hot.

Note
You can experiment with how the taste and texture of these fritters is altered by temperature contrasts by serving the hot fritters with banana ice cream. It's delicious!

Banana ice cream

This recipe uses double cream and lots of egg yolks to make a classic high-fat custard that retains its creamy texture when frozen. The alcohol makes it softer and more scoopable. It's perfect for very ripe bananas.

Place the cream and vanilla pod in a medium saucepan. Set over a low heat and bring to the boil, then remove from the heat.

Purée the bananas with the lemon juice and rum, with a hand-held blender or in a food processor. Set aside in a bowl large enough to hold the custard as well.

Whisk the egg yolks with the sugar, until pale and fluffy. Slowly stir the hot cream into the egg yolks with a wooden spoon. Return the mixture to the pan.

Set over a low heat and, using a wooden spoon, stir continuously in a figure-of-eight motion until the cream thickens enough to coat the back of the spoon. This will take 10–20 minutes, depending on your confidence. Don't let it boil or the custard will split. If it feels as though it's getting too hot, just lift the pan off the heat and keep stirring. As soon as it is ready, strain the custard through a sieve into the banana purée. Mix well, cover and, once cool, chill in the refrigerator.

Churn the cold custard, according to the instructions for your ice cream machine, until it reaches a soft set. Transfer to a covered container and store in the freezer. Alternatively, pour into a shallow plastic container, cover and freeze. Beat with a fork every 40 minutes, or until you have a smooth, soft-set ice cream.

Sue Quinn

Cocoa hazelnut traybake with espresso Swiss meringue

The chocolate, coffee and hazelnut notes combine in delicious harmony here to make an indulgent and deeply flavourful cake. The intensely chocolatey sponge is topped with espresso-spiked meringue and sprinkled with toasted hazelnuts for crunch. Perfect served with good strong coffee.

Makes one 20cm x 20cm traybake

For the cake

100ml vegetable oil, plus extra to brush the tin

100g blanched skinned hazelnuts

80g plain flour

20g cornflour

45g cocoa powder

1½ tsp baking powder

1 tsp bicarbonate of soda

160g soft dark brown sugar

130ml buttermilk

2 large eggs

1 tsp vanilla extract

For the meringue

2 large egg whites

110g caster sugar

2 tsp espresso coffee powder, or to taste

Heat your oven to 180°C/160°C fan. Oil a 20cm x 20cm brownie tin or baking dish and line the base with baking paper.

Lightly toast the hazelnuts in a dry frying pan, shaking frequently, until golden. Cool a little, then blitz half of them in a small blender or spice grinder to a powder. Roughly chop the remaining hazelnuts and set aside.

To make the cake, combine both the flours, the blitzed hazelnuts, cocoa powder, baking powder, bicarbonate of soda, sugar and a pinch of salt in a large bowl. Whisk well so everything is thoroughly combined, with no lumps.

In a separate bowl, whisk together the oil, buttermilk, eggs, vanilla and 70ml hot water. Pour into the flour mixture and whisk until smooth and glossy.

Pour into the prepared tin and bake for 30–35 minutes, or until firm to touch and an inserted skewer comes out clean. Leave in the tin for 10 minutes, then turn out onto a wire rack and carefully peel off the baking paper.

When the cake has cooled completely, make the meringue. Place the egg whites and sugar into a heatproof bowl and stir to combine.

Set the bowl over a pan of gently simmering water – don't let the water touch the bottom of the bowl – and whisk constantly until the sugar has dissolved and the mixture reads 80°C on a confectionary thermometer or probe.

Carefully remove the bowl from the pan and using electric beaters, whip until thick, glossy and cool. Sprinkle over the espresso powder and beat to incorporate.

Spread the meringue over the cake in lovely swirls and scatter the chopped toasted hazelnuts over the top. Serve immediately.

Claudia Roden

Dried fruit compote with custard:
zurracapote con crema pastelera vasca

Zurracapote, also called *marmelada de frutos secos,* is a New Year's Eve special in the Basque country and in Navarre. It is great served with the Basque custard below that can be flavoured with rum or Cognac.

Serves 6

250g prunes
250g dried peaches or apricots
250ml red wine
250ml water
100g sugar
100g lightly toasted flaked almonds or coarsely chopped walnuts

For the *crema pastelera vasca*
500ml whole milk
6 large egg yolks
175g sugar
3 tbsp plain flour
3–4 tbsp rum

Soak the dried fruits in water for 2 hours, then drain and put them in a pan with the wine, water and sugar and simmer, covered, for 20 – 30 minutes, until they are very soft.

For the *crema pastelera vasca*, bring the milk to the boil in a heavy bottomed pan. In a bowl beat the egg yolks with the sugar to a light pale cream with an electric hand beater, then beat in the flour.

Gradually pour in the milk, a little at a time, beating vigorously until well blended. Then pour the mixture back into the pan. Stir constantly with a wooden spoon or spatula over very low heat until the custard thickens. If any lumps form at the start they will disappear as you work the custard vigorously. Add the rum and mix well.

Serve cold in little bowls, the custard at the bottom, the cooked fruits on top with their wine sauce sprinkled with almonds or walnuts.

Chantelle Nicholson

Foraged blackberry and fig leaf upside-down pudding

This pudding is the epitome of a late summer treat. The plump, juiciness of the tart blackberries with the soft, sponge-like pudding make a wonderful combination. Add in the fragranced fig leaf syrup and you have a lovely way to finish off any meal.

Vegan

Serves 4 – 6

200g foraged blackberries

For the sponge

150g aquafaba (canned chickpea brine)

150g caster sugar

150g plain flour

1½ tsp baking powder

50g ground almonds

80g non-dairy butter, melted

For the fig leaf syrup

100g caster sugar

100ml water

50ml vodka

3 large fig leaves, roughly chopped

yoghurt or ice cream, to serve

Preheat the oven to 190°C/170°C fan. Grease an 18cm cake tin well with some of the melted butter.

Arrange the blackberries in the bottom of the cake tin.

For the sponge, whisk the aquafaba in a bowl with an electric whisk, or using a stand mixer, until stiff. Whilst still whisking, gradually add the caster sugar. Whisk until stiff and glossy. Place the flour, baking powder and ground almonds into a bowl, mix well. Fold in the aquafaba meringue then gently mix through the melted butter. Pour the batter on top of the blackberries and gently smooth over. Bake for 15–20 minutes until a skewer inserted comes out clean.

Whilst the pudding is baking, bring the sugar and water to the boil until the sugar has dissolved. Remove from the heat and add the vodka and fig leaves. Blend together for 2 minutes until the leaves have broken down and you have a fragrant, green-hued syrup. Pass through a fine sieve into a jug.

Prick the top of the sponge all over with a skewer then pour some of the hot syrup over the hot sponge. Allow to sit for 10 minutes before turning out and inverting the pudding.

Serve with the remaining fig syrup and with your favourite yoghurt or ice cream.

Pam Corbin
Rosaceae jelly

This delightful jelly combines the fruit, flowers and fragrance from three well-loved members of the attractive Rosaceae, or the rose family. All have an equally important part in its making. Apples bring pectin and acidity to help it gel, raspberries their intense flavour and fruitiness, whilst the rose petals their beautiful colour and fragrance.

Choose deeply scented, richly coloured red or pink rose petals – gather the petals when you can and pop them in an airtight bag and freeze until you have sufficient. Alternatively, and if you don't have access to scented rose petals, you can add one or two tablespoons of rose water at the end of cooking. Enjoy with freshly baked scones and clotted cream; spoon into creamy rice pud or use to glaze fruit tarts.

Vegan
Makes 3 x 200ml jars

600g sharp cooking apples
50g–100g fragrant rose petals
½ unwaxed lemon, roughly chopped
1 tbsp white wine vinegar
500g raspberries, fresh or frozen
500g granulated sugar

Place a couple of small saucers in the fridge to check for setting point.

There's no need to peel or core the apples – just rinse and chop them up into chunks. Put the apples in a roomy pan with the rose petals, lemon, vinegar and 800ml cold water. Cover and bring to a simmer for 15 minutes or until the apples are beginning to soften. Add the raspberries crushing them down with a spoon, and continue to cook for another 10 minutes or so, or until the apples and raspberries have broken down to a soft pulp. Remove from the heat.

Strain the cooked mixture through a scalded jelly bag or a large sieve lined with muslin set over a bowl. Leave to drip through for several hours or overnight – the longer the better. To hurry things you can place a small saucer on the surface of the fruit, with a weight on top – a jar of jam works well!

Pour the raspberry stock into a measuring jug discarding any sediment from the bottom of the bowl – you should have approximately 750ml (top it up with a little extra water if you need to). Pour the stock into a large heavy-based pan or preserving pan and bring to a brisk boil for 3–4 minutes.

Reduce the heat and sprinkle in the sugar, a third at a time, stirring each time until it has dissolved. Then increase the heat to a brisk boil for 8–10 minutes until setting point is reached (see overleaf). Remove from the heat.

Rest the jelly for a minute or two. If a jelly has formed a skin, carefully remove it with a slotted spoon or jam skimmer. Tip the jelly into a wide-necked jug with a good pouring lip, then fill into sterilised jars to the brim and seal immediately with a twist on lid.

Testing for setting point

Remove the pan from the heat. Drop a little of the hot preserve onto a cold plate. Leave to one side or pop it in the fridge for a minute or so to cool, then lightly push your finger through to see if it comes together in a small gel that holds it shape and doesn't just pool away. Any gel should be light and delicate and not all sticky. If the mixture remains runny, return the pan to the heat for a couple more minutes, then test again.

Signe Johansen
Almond and hazelnut torte with roasted plums and blackberries

This all-star torte tastes wonderful at any time of the year but really comes into its own in late summer and early autumn when seasonal fruit such as blackberries, plums and apples are at their peak.

Serves 6–8

125g butter, softened

175g golden caster sugar

1 tsp vanilla extract

3 medium eggs

3 tbsp plain flour (or gluten-free flour)

125g ground almonds

125g ground hazelnuts

1 tsp baking powder

¼ tsp fine sea salt

handful of fresh blackberries

For the roasted plums

1 plum per person

demerara sugar

cinnamon

Preheat the oven to 170ºC/150ºC fan and lightly grease or line a 23cm round cake tin with baking parchment.

Cream the butter, sugar and vanilla extract together in a medium-large bowl until pale and fluffy. Slice the plums in half and place in a small baking tray or roasting tin, sprinkle a little demerara sugar and cinnamon over each plum and set aside.

When the butter is creamy, add in the eggs, one egg and one tablespoon of flour at a time, mixing well between each egg.

Add the ground nuts along with the baking powder and fine sea salt to the mixture and stir until just blended.

Pour/scoop this mixture into your prepared cake tin and place both this and the tin with the halved plums on the same middle shelf of the oven and bake for 30 minutes, or until the cake has risen, looks golden brown and feels firm to the touch. If need be, remove the plums before the cake is done. They should look soft and oozing a little of their juice.

Remove the cake tin from the oven, cool on a wire rack before turning out. Serve with the roasted plums and fresh blackberries as garnish, adding a scoop of ice cream or creme fraiche if you feel like it.

Alternatives: add blackberries, blackcurrants, redcurrants or any berries you like to the torte mixture and bake together if you prefer. This torte is also delicious accompanied with rhubarb, apple and citrus fruits.

Claire Ptak

Orange, ginger and rye upside-down cake

Everyone loves to eat upside-down cakes because the ratio of fruit to sponge is just so perfect. It can be served warm (my personal favourite) or made ahead of time and served at room temperature. This version is spicy and rich with the beautiful brightness of citrus on top (bottom!). When I think of Kew Gardens, I think of those incredible glasshouses and of all the oranges grown in them since Victorian times.

Serves 8–10

For the oranges
50g unsalted butter
125g demerara sugar
1 vanilla pod, split
6–8 oranges of any type

For the sponge
300g dark rye flour
½ tsp fine salt
1 tsp ground ginger
1 tsp ground cinnamon
1 tsp mixed spice
½ tsp ground cloves
200g unsalted butter
200g light brown sugar
200g black treacle
160g whole milk
2 eggs

Preheat the oven to 180ºC/160ºC fan and have ready a 25cm solid-bottomed cake tin.

In a small saucepan, melt the butter and the demerara sugar. Split the vanilla pod, scrape the seeds into the butter and break up with a fork, then pour the mixture into the cake tin and swirl to coat, laying the split vanilla pod in the bottom.

Cut off the ends of the oranges and cut downwards around the fruit to peel. Slice crossways into 1½cm slices. Arrange the slices in the bottom of the cake tin on top of the vanilla pod.

To make the sponge, whisk the flour, salt and spices together in a bowl. Set aside. In a small saucepan, melt the unsalted butter, sugar and treacle. Whisk together until smooth. Carefully mix this into the dry flour mix.

Whisk in the milk and finally the eggs. Pour the cake mixture over the oranges and bake in the oven for 45–55 minutes or until springy and a skewer inserted comes out clean.

Let the cake cool for 15 minutes in the tin, then use a knife to release the cake from the edge of the tin. Put a plate over the cake and turn it upside-down so that the bottom becomes the top.

Serve with plain yoghurt to keep it light, or a little creme fraiche for an excellent afternoon treat.

Contributors

Zoe Adjonyoh is a chef, writer, entrepreneur, founder of Zoe's Ghana Kitchen and has pioneered modern West African food through supper clubs, a restaurant, and events since 2010. She is the author of the much-lauded cookbook *Zoe's Ghana Kitchen*. She recently joined the James Beard Foundation in New York City as the Director of Women's Programs.

Brwa Ahmad was born in Kurdistan, and at the age of 15 moved to London. He's currently the Executive Chef at Kew Gardens. His focus at Kew is learning about sustainable food and under-utilised ingredients from around the world and creating new food experiences for visitors to Kew as well as spreading the sustainability message.

MiMi Aye is the author of the award-winning *Mandalay*, described by Nigella Lawson as 'wonderful', by Jay Rayner as 'a gorgeous book [that] schooled me lightly in a culinary Burma', and by Tom Parker-Bowles as 'a glorious revelation'. She hosts 'The MSG Pod' and is on social media as @meemalee.

Kimiko Barber began her cooking and food writing career at Books for Cooks, London over 20 years ago. Her first book, *Sushi: Taste and Technique* was published in its revised second edition in 2017. She divides her time between London and rural Oxfordshire where she keeps honey bees and grows vegetables.

Raymond Blanc is acknowledged as one of the finest chefs in the world. Chef patron of Le Manoir aux Quat'Saisons, A Belmond Hotel, Oxfordshire, his restaurant has retained two Michelin stars for over 37 years. He has starred in numerous TV series and written several cookbooks, the latest being *Simply Raymond: Recipes from Home*.

Vanessa Bolosier learnt most of what she knows about cooking from her Martiniquan dad in the family kitchen in Guadeloupe. She moved to London in 2005 and embarked on a mission to spread the love, sunshine and joy that Caribbean Creole food brings. She is the author of the *Sunshine Kitchen* cookbook.

Carla Capalbo was born in New York and brought up in London and Paris. She lived in Italy for over 20 years and recently has focused her attention on the gastronomy of Georgia in the Caucasus. Her award-winning books include food and wine guides to Georgia, Collio, Tuscany and Naples and Campania. www.carlacapalbo.com

Jenny Chandler is a Bristol-based food writer and teacher who's passionate about getting more plants on plates. Author of half a dozen cookbooks, including *Pulse* and *Green Kids Cook*, Jenny runs sustainable cooking workshops with chefs, home cooks and children. In 2016 she was UN FAO European Ambassador for the International Year of Pulses.

Xanthe Clay has written for *The Telegraph* for 22 years, and pops up from time to time in other media including *delicious.* magazine and BBC Radio 4. She was President of the Guild of Food Writers 2014–2018 and is currently Academy Chair (UK and Ireland) for The World's 50 Best Restaurants.

Felicity Cloake is the award-winning author of *The Guardian*'s long-running *How to Make the Perfect* column as well as six books, including *One More Croissant for the Road*, (shortlisted for the Fortnum & Mason food book of the year award) and *Red Sauce, Brown Sauce: a British Breakfast Odyssey*.

Angela Clutton is an award-winning food writer and presenter. Her debut book *The Vinegar Cupboard* won four awards and she is currently working on her next book. Angela also presents the Borough Market podcast 'Borough Talks' and is the Director of the British Library Food Season.

Pam Corbin gained her wealth of expertise in preserving foods when she owned Thursday Cottage, a small artisan preserves company producing exceptionally good jams, marmalades and curds. She has written the bestselling River Cottage Handbooks on *Preserves* and *Cakes* and her latest book *The Book of Preserves* was published in 2019.

Mark Diacono is an award-winning food writer, lucky enough to spend most of his time growing, eating, writing and talking about food. He has written and photographed 13 books, winning Food Book of the Year twice, and was shortlisted in 2020 for a James Beard Foundation award for his book *Sour*.

Timothy d'Offay became fascinated by tea culture while living in Kyoto over 25 years ago, and started to explore the tea traditions of Japan, Taiwan and Korea. This led him to start importing tea in the late 1990s and to found Postcard Teas in 2005. He has also written several books on tea.

Anja Dunk is a cook, writer and artist. The food she cooks is influenced by her family history, the seasons and the bounty of produce that grows wild in the countryside.

Fuchsia Dunlop is an award-winning cook and food writer specialising in Chinese cuisine. She trained as a chef at the Sichuan Higher Institute of Cuisine and is the author of six books, including the memoir *Shark's Fin and Sichuan Pepper*, and, most recently, *The Food of Sichuan*.

Hattie Ellis is an award-winning author and journalist who writes about practical ways to eat sustainably and the people, places and culture that make food such a rich part of life.

Monica Galetti was born in Samoa and raised in Wellington, New Zealand, and trained as a chef. After working for 12 years at two Michelin-starred Le Gavroche, London she opened her own restaurant Mere in London in 2017. She is a familiar television personality from 'MasterChef: The Professionals' and 'Amazing Hotels' and is the author of three books.

Irina Georgescu is a Romanian food writer and author who lives in the UK, and writes about the traditions and history of her country's culinary landscape. Her books focus on the cultural diversity of Romania and on its many influences that came to shape today's national cuisine.

Helen Goh is a recipe developer and co-author of *Sweet*, written with Yotam Ottolenghi. She is based in London but writes a baking column for *The Sydney Morning Herald* and *The Age* in Australia.

Roopa Gulati lived in India for two decades, working as a chef at the Taj Hotel and as a writer and broadcaster. On her return to the UK, she was Food Editor at UKTV's Good Food Channel and is now a freelance recipe and feature writer and the author of *India: The World Vegetarian*.

Luiz Hara left investment banking in 2011 and retrained as a Chef under Le Cordon Bleu London's Grande Diplomê. He has been hosting a Japanese & Nikkei Supperclub at his Islington home ever since and is the author of *Nikkei Cuisine* and *The Japanese Larder* cookbooks. Connect with Luiz @thelondonfoodie.

Diana Henry is a bestselling writer and journalist. She is the acclaimed author of 12 books and has won awards from the Andre Simon Memorial Fund, the James Beard Foundation, Fortnum & Mason and the Guild of Food Writers. She has had a weekly column in *The Sunday Telegraph* for 18 years.

Olia Hercules was born in Ukraine and has forged a career as a chef in the UK. She is the author of the critically acclaimed *Mamushka*, *Kaukasis* and the recently published *Summer Kitchens*, which explores the people, landscape and recipes that continue to beckon her home.

Ken Hom OBE is the man who showed the British how to cook Asian food. A leading authority on Chinese cuisine, he is a highly respected, much-loved and celebrated TV chef. He is the author of nearly 40 books, which have inspired millions of home cooks around the world.

Simon Hopkinson is Lancashire-born and made his name as an acclaimed young chef in London, first at Hilaire, then at Terence Conran's Bibendum. He is a highly regarded, much-loved food writer, sharing his knowledge of cooking through newspaper columns, 'The Good Cook' TV series and cookbooks, among them his award-winning *Roast Chicken and Other Stories*.

Ching-He Huang MBE is an International, Emmy nominated TV chef and bestselling cookery author who has become an ambassador of Chinese cooking around the world. Her creative food ethos is to use fresh, organic and ethically sourced ingredients to create modern dishes with Chinese heritage, fusing tradition and innovation.

Tom Hunt is an award-winning chef, writer, climate change campaigner and author of new cookbook *Eating for Pleasure, People & Planet*. He writes a weekly recipe column for *The Guardian* called *Waste Not*, works closely with various charities including Fairtrade and The Soil Association and is a signatory to the Chef's Manifesto.

Rukmini Iyer is the bestselling author of *The Roasting Tin* series, selling over a million copies worldwide. Her books *Roasting Tin*, *The Green Roasting Tin*, *The Quick Roasting Tin*, *The Roasting Tin Around the World*, *Green Barbecue*, *Sweet Roasting Tin* and *India Express* are all transforming how Britain cooks. www.instagram.com/missminifer

Signe Johansen is a Norwegian-American food and drink writer based in London. Author of *Spirited*, *Solo* and two *Scandilicious* books, she's also written books with titles that don't begin with S, like *How to Hygge* and is a co-author of *The Ultimate Student Cookbook*. Follow her online @signesjohansen and signejohansen.substack.com

Hugh Johnson is an award-winning London and Italy-based food and drink photographer whose passion for making the everyday appear beautiful allows his work to be both familiar and intriguing. His portfolio celebrates simple combinations that work. He has won many international awards and was recently awarded Fortnum & Mason Photographer of the Year.

Anna Jones is a cook, writer, the voice of modern vegetarian cooking and the author of the bestselling *A Modern Way to Eat*, *A Modern Way to Cook*, *The Modern Cook's Year*, and most recently, *One*. Anna believes that vegetables should be put at the centre of every table.

Sybil Kapoor is an influential award-winning food and travel writer. Her book *Sight Smell Touch Taste Sound: A New Way to Cook* was the first to explore how sensory perception changes how you cook. It was voted the Fortnum & Mason Cookery Book of the Year in 2018.

Asma Khan is the chef and owner of Darjeeling Express, an award-winning cookbook author and PhD in British Constitutional Law at King's College London. Asma is the first British chef to feature in Netflix's Emmy nominated 'Chef's Table' and the first chef featured on *Vogue*'s list of 25 most influential women for 2020.

Tessa Kiros is half Finnish and half Greek Cypriot, born in London and raised in South Africa. She has published nine books including *Falling Cloudberries* and *Food From Many Greek Kitchens* and is still inspired by traditional cuisines and cultures around the world. She lives in Tuscany with her husband and two daughters.

Florence Knight was head chef at Polpetto, a Venetian-inspired restaurant in London, for five years. In 2013 she published her first cookbook *One: A Cook and Her Cupboard*. Florence is now the Executive Chef of Sessions Arts Club, Clerkenwell, where she has received critical acclaim for her menu inspired by British, French and Italian cooking.

Liz Knight is a leading wild food expert, the author of *Forage: Wild Plants to Gather, Cook and Eat*. She teaches foraging courses in the Welsh / English borders and runs Forage Fine Foods, a wild food business. Her ambrosial recipes have led many sceptics to eat their words and their weeds.

Lara Lee is the author of Indonesian cookbook *Coconut & Sambal* which was named one of the best cookbooks of the year by *The New York Times*, *The Guardian*, *Eater*, *National Geographic* and many more. She is a regular contributor for Food52, NYT Cooking, Bon Appetit, Food & Wine and *The Guardian*.

Dan Lepard is one of the world's leading bakers, the go-to guy for two generations of young cooks. His cookbooks, including *Baking With Passion*, *The Handmade Loaf* and *Short & Sweet*, have garnered plaudits and won awards and encouraged people around the world to bake at home.

Elisabeth Luard is a food writer who took inspiration for her earlier career as a natural history artist from childhood visits to Kew Gardens. While bringing up her family in Andalucia through the 1970s, she worked on the botany of Ronda. She continues to paint, draw and write and contributes a cookery column to *The Oldie* magazine.

Uyen Luu is the author of *Vietnamese* and *My Vietnamese Kitchen*. Running for over a decade, Uyen started her Vietnamese supper club in 2009 and teaches Vietnamese home cooking. Uyen is a food photographer, lives in London and continues to create and write Vietnamese recipes.

Chetna Makan was born in India, and now lives in the UK. Since appearing on 'The Great British Bake Off', she has written five cookbooks on baking, Indian street food, healthy Indian food, vegetarian and quick Indian food. She has a popular YouTube channel 'Food with Chetna' where she shares her creative flair for cooking and baking.

Christine McFadden, Dorset-based food writer and author of more than 16 cookbooks, is an avid supporter of local food producers and is passionate about encouraging awareness of traditional foods in danger of extinction. She is also an enthusiastic gardener-cook who enjoys growing herbs, vegetables and unusual salad greens.

Thomasina Miers is a cook, writer, TV presenter, 'MasterChef' winner, and mother of three. She co-founded her first restaurant Wahaca in 2007, going on to open 17 more, all of which are carbon neutral. She received an OBE in 2019 for services to the food industry and has a weekly recipe column in *The Guardian*.

Martin Allen Morales is an award-winning social enterprise and business leader. He is the author of the bestselling *Ceviche* and *Andina* cookbooks and led these restaurants, paving the way for sustainable and nutritious Peruvian food in Britain. Having ran companies for Apple and Disney he now runs the education charity The Institute of Imagination.

Chantelle Nicholson is a multi-award-winning chef and restaurateur. As chef-owner of Apricity restaurant in Mayfair, London, she is an advocate for seasonality and sustainability, championing veg-forward cooking and committed to creating a more sustainable future across her operation and activities. She is the author of *Planted*, a plant-based cookbook.

Jill Norman's culinary career began when she created the food list for Penguin Books. In the process she learned to appreciate and to cook foods from around the world. She is acknowledged internationally as an authority on herbs and spices. Her books have been translated and won awards in many countries.

Zaleha Kadir Olpin grew up in Malaysia and was taught to cook traditional Malaysian dishes by her mother from an early age. She wrote the award-winning cookbook *My Rendang Isn't Crispy*. She runs the Malaysian Kitchen UK, teaches Malaysian cookery and produces her own spice paste under the brand name 'That Rendang Lady'.

Yotam Ottolenghi is the restaurateur and chef-patron of the Ottolenghi delis, NOPI and ROVI restaurants. He is the author of eight bestselling cookery books and writes weekly columns for *The Guardian*. He is known for championing vegetables, and ingredients once seen as 'exotic', to create meals which are full of colour, flavour and sunshine.

Sarit Packer and Itamar Srulovich opened Middle Eastern restaurant Honey & Co in London in 2012, followed by grill house Honey & Smoke, and deli Honey & Spice. They have written four cookbooks, write a weekly recipe column for *FT Weekend Magazine* and host a podcast, 'Honey & Co: The Food Sessions'.

Selina Periampillai is a London-based self-taught chef, born to Mauritian parents. She hosted the first Mauritian supperclub from her home in London and now caters events, teaches cookery classes and does cookery demos to share her knowledge of Mauritian cuisine. She is the author of *The Island Kitchen* cookbook.

Catherine Phipps is a London-based food writer and cookery book author, with special interests in sustainable food and pressure cooking. Her most recent published works include *Citrus* and *Leaf*, and her latest book is *Modern Pressure Cooking*.

Thane Prince is a food writer of 30 years standing. She has published 14 books, appeared in a myriad of television and radio programmes. She ran an award-winning cookery school in Aldeburgh, Suffolk and now lives, cooks and eats in London.

Claire Ptak is a Californian who has lived in London since 2005. She is the owner of Violet Bakery and works extensively as a food writer and stylist. Ptak was commissioned to make the royal wedding cake for Prince Harry and Meghan Markle in 2018 and is now working on her latest cookbook.

Sue Quinn is an award-winning food writer and cookbook author. She regularly writes for the BBC, *The Telegraph*, *The Sunday Times* and *delicious.* magazine, and her recipes have appeared in all of the leading British food publications. Sue has written 14 cookbooks and her latest, *Cocoa,* was published in 2019 to wide acclaim.

Rachel Roddy lives in Rome with her Sicilian partner and son. She is the author of three cookbooks, *Five Quarters* (which won the Andre Simon Award), *Two Kitchens* and *An A to Z of Pasta*. She has a weekly column in *The Guardian* called *A Kitchen in Rome*.

Claudia Roden, born in Egypt, writes about Middle Eastern and Mediterranean food. Her books have won her many awards. Her latest, *Med,* is what she cooks today for family and friends. The recipes are inspired by magic moments and remembered dishes over decades of travels researching Mediterranean regional home cooking.

Niki Segnit's first book, *The Flavour Thesaurus*, won the André Simon Award for best food book. It has been translated into 15 languages. Nigella Lawson called Segnit's second book, *Lateral Cooking*, 'a staggering achievement' and Brian Eno described it as 'astonishing and addictive'. It has been translated into nine languages.

Sefanit Sophie Sirak-Kebede is a trained hotelier who holds decades of experience in the food and drink industry, training and working in Ethiopia, Germany, Switzerland, and the UK. Alongside her husband, Menyahill, she now owns Tobia Teff, a London-based family-run business specialising in 100% pure teff products including teff flour, teff breads and teff snack bars.

Kathy Slack is a cook, vegetable grower and author who previously worked at Daylesford Organic Farm. She also hosts supper clubs and cookery demonstrations with harvests from her garden. Kathy has won the Young British Foodie award, a Soil Association award and a Guild of Food Writers award. Find her recipes at kathyslack.com

Ed Smith (@rocketandsquash) is a cook and food writer. A former City lawyer, Ed retrained as a chef before settling into pop-ups, consulting, recipe development and writing. He is the author of the award-winning food blog rocketandsquash.com and three acclaimed cookbooks: *Crave*, *On the Side*, and *The Borough Market Cookbook.*

Meera Sodha is a voracious home cook, who writes a weekly column for *The Guardian*. She has written three cookbooks: *Made In India* (named a book of the year by *The Times* and the *Financial Times*), *Fresh India*, which won the 2017 *Observer Food Monthly*'s Best New Cookbook Award and *East*.

Rosie Sykes is a chef, writer and consultant. She has worked with some of the leading names in British food. She had her own pub in central London and has helped establish kitchens for restaurants, delis and hotels nationwide. Rosie has written three cookery books and now works mainly on community projects.

Sami Tamimi is a chef and award-winning author, and is one of the business partners that founded Ottolenghi. Alongside Yotam Ottolenghi and Tara Wigley, Sami is co-author of three bestselling cookbooks: *Ottolenghi: The Cookbook*, *Jerusalem* and *Falastin: A Cookbook*.

Claire Thomson is a professional chef, food writer, columnist for *The Telegraph* and the author of seven cook books. Claire also posts on instagram as @5oclockapron documenting what she cooks, day in, day out.

Sumayya Usmani is an author and educator with a focus on food writing and intuitive cooking. Born and raised in Pakistan, her recipes highlight her heritage. She is the author of *Summers Under the Tamarind Tree* and *Mountain Berries and Dessert Spice*. Sumayya's next book, a food memoir, will be published in 2023.

Özlem Warren is a native of Turkey and author of *Özlem's Turkish Table: Recipes from my Homeland*. She is passionate about her homeland's cuisine and has been teaching Turkish cookery in the UK, USA and Jordan for over 15 years. She has a popular Turkish recipe blog, Özlem's Turkish Table (www.ozlemsturkishtable.com).

Da-Hae West is a Korean cookery teacher, consultant and author of *Eat Korean*. She has considerable experience of promoting Korean food, a close relationship with the Korean Cultural Centre and experience working on TV productions 'Gizzi Erskine's Seoul Food', and 'John Torode's Korean Food Tour'. For her cookery classes, visit www.dahaewest.com.

Recommended reading

Zoe Adjonyoh. *Zoe's Ghana Kitchen*. Mitchell Beazley, London (2017).

Alexandre Antonelli. *The Hidden Universe: Adventures in Biodiversity*. Ebury Press in association with the Royal Botanic Gardens, Kew (2022).

MiMi Aye. *Mandalay: Recipes and Tales from a Burmese Kitchen*. Bloomsbury Absolute, London (2019).

Kimiko Barber. *Cook Japanese at Home*. Kyle Books, London (2017).

Raymond Blanc. *Simply Raymond: Recipes from Home*. Headline Home, London (2021).

Vanessa Bolosier. *Sunshine Kitchen: Delicious Creole Recipes from the Heart of the Caribbean*. Pavilion, London (2021).

Carla Capalbo. *Tasting Georgia: A Food and Wine Journey in the Caucasus*. Pallas Athene, London (2020).

Jenny Chandler. *Pulse: Truly Modern Recipes for Beans, Chickpeas & Lentils to Tempt Meat Eaters and Vegetarians Alike*. Pavilion, London (2019).

Xanthe Clay. *Recipes to Know by Heart*. Mitchell Beazley, London (2008).

Felicity Cloake. *Completely Perfect: 120 Essential Recipes for Every Cook*. Penguin Books, London (2018).

Angela Clutton. *The Vinegar Cupboard: Recipes and History of an Everyday Ingredient*. Bloomsbury Absolute, London (2019).

Pam Corbin. *Pam the Jam: The Book of Preserves*. Bloomsbury, London (2019).

Mark Diacono. *Herb: A Cook's Companion*. Hardie Grant, London (2021).

Timothy d'Offay. *Easy Leaf Tea: Tea House Recipes to Make at Home*. Ryland Peters & Small, London (2017).

Hélèna Dove. *The Kew Gardener's Guide to Growing Vegetables*. Frances Lincoln, London in association with the Royal Botanic Gardens, Kew (2020).

Anja Dunk. *Strudel, Noodles and Dumplings: The New Taste of German Cooking*. Fourth Estate, London (2018).

Fuchsia Dunlop. *The Food of Sichuan*. Bloomsbury, London (2019).

Hattie Ellis. *Spoonfuls of Honey*. Pavilion, London (2019).

Holly Farrell. *The Kew Gardener's Guide to Growing Herbs*. White Lion Publishing, London in association with the Royal Botanic Gardens, Kew (2019).

Monica Galetti. *At Home*. Aster, London (2021).

Irina Georgescu. *Tava: Eastern European Baking and Desserts from Romania and Beyond*. Hardie Grant, London (2022).

Roopa Gulati. *India: The World Vegetarian*. Bloomsbury Absolute, London (2020).

Luiz Hara. *Nikkei Cuisine: Japanese Food the South American Way*. Jaqui Small LLP, London (2015).

Diana Henry. *How to Eat a Peach*. Mitchell Beazley, London (2018).

Olia Hercules. *Summer Kitchens: Recipes and Reminiscences from Every Corner of Ukraine*. Bloomsbury, London (2020).

Ken Hom. *My Stir-Fried Life*. The Robson Press, London (2016).

Simon Hopkinson. *The Vegetarian Option*. Reissued edition. Quadrille, London (2018)

Ching-He Huang. *Asian Green*. Kyle Books, London (2021).

Tom Hunt. *Eating for People, Pleasure & Planet*. Kyle Books, London (2020).

Rukmini Iyer. *India Express*. Square Peg, London (2022).

Signe Johansen. S*olo: The Joy of Cooking for One*. Bluebird Books for Life, London (2018).

Anna Jones. *One: Pot, Pan, Planet*. Fourth Estate, London (2021).

Sybil Kapoor. *Sight Smell Touch Taste Sound - A New Way to Cook*. Pavilion, London (2018).

Kew Pocketbooks: Fruit. Royal Botanic Gardens, Kew (2022).

Kew Pocketbooks: Herbs & Spices. Royal Botanic Gardens, Kew (2022).

Asma Khan. *Ammu: Indian Home Cooking to Nourish Your Soul*. Ebury Press, London (2022).

Tessa Kiros. *Limoncello and Linen Water*. Murdoch Books, London and Sydney (2012).

Florence Knight. *One: A Cook and Her Cupboard*. Headline Home, London (2013).

Liz Knight. *Forage: Wild Plants to Gather and Eat*. Laurence King Publishing, London (2021).

Lara Lee. *Coconut & Sambal: Recipes from my Indonesian Kitchen*. Bloomsbury, London (2020).

Dan Lepard. *Short & Sweet*. Fourth Estate, London (2011).

Jenny Linford. *The Missing Ingredient: The Curious Role of Time in Food and Flavour*. Penguin Books, London (2019).

Elisabeth Luard. *The Flavours of Andalucia*. Grub Street Publishing, London (2017).

Uyen Luu. *Vietnamese: Simple Vietnamese Food to Cook at Home*. Hardie Grant, London (2021).

Chetna Makan. *Chetna's 30-Minute Indian: Quick and Easy Everyday Meals*. Mitchell Beazley, London (2021).

Christine McFadden. *Pepper: The Spice that Changed the World*. Absolute Press, London (2008).

Thomasina Miers. *Meat-Free Mexican*. Hodder & Stoughton, London (2022).

Martin Morales. *Andina: The Heart of Peruvian Food: Recipes and Stories from the Andes*. Quadrille, London (2017).

Chantelle Nicholson. *Planted: A Chef's Show-Stopping Vegan Recipes.* Kyle Books, London (2018).

Jill Norman. *Herbs & Spices, The Cook's Reference.* Dorling Kindersley, London (2002).

Zaleha Kadir Olpin. *My Rendang Isn't Crispy and Other Favourite Malaysian Dishes*. Marshall Cavendish International, Singapore (2019).

Yotam Ottolenghi and Helen Goh. *Sweet.* Ebury Press, London (2017).

Yotam Ottolenghi and Noor Murad. *Ottolenghi Test Kitchen: Shelf Love*. Ebury Press, London (2021).

Sarit Packer and Itamar Srulovich. *Chasing Smoke: Cooking Over Fire Around the Levant.* Pavilion, London (2021).

Selina Periampillai. *The Island Kitchen: Recipes from Mauritius and the Indian Ocean*. Bloomsbury, London (2019).

Catherine Phipps. *Leaf: Lettuce, Greens, Herbs, Weeds: Over 120 Recipes that Celebrate Varied, Versatile Leaves*. Quadrille, London (2019).

Thane Prince. *Ham, Pickles and Jam: Traditional Skills for the Modern Kitchen Larder*. Pavilion, London (2011).

Claire Ptak. *The Violet Bakery Cookbook*. Square Peg, London (2015).

Sue Quinn. *Cocoa: An Exploration of Chocolate, with Recipes*. Quadrille, London (2019).

Rachel Roddy. *An A to Z of Pasta: Stories, Shapes, Sauces, Recipes*. Fig Tree, London (2021).

Claudia Roden. *Med: A Cookbook*. Ebury Press, London (2021).

Dan Saladino. *Eating to Extinction: The World's Rarest Foods and Why We Need to Save Them*. Jonathan Cape, London (2021).

Niki Segnit. *The Flavour Thesaurus*. Bloomsbury, London (2010).

Kathy Slack. *From the Veg Patch: 10 Favourite Vegetables, 100 Simple Recipes Everyone Will Love.* Ebury Press, London (2021).

Ed Smith. *Crave: Recipes Arranged by Flavour, to Suit Your Mood and Appetite.* Quadrille, London (2021).

Meera Sodha. *East: 120 Vegan and Vegetarian Recipes from Bangalore to Beijing.* Fig Tree, London (2019).

Tim Spector. *Spoon Fed: Why Almost Everything We've Been Told About Food is Wrong.* Vintage, London (2022).

Rosie Sykes. *The Sunday Night Book: 52 Short Recipes to Make the Weekend Feel Longer.* Hardie Grant, London (2017).

Sami Tamimi and Tara Wigley. *Falastin: A Cookbook.* Ebury Press, London (2021).

Claire Thomson. *Tomato: 80 Recipes Celebrating the Extraordinary Tomato.* Quadrille, London (2022).

Sumayya Usmani. *Summers Under the Tamarind Tree: Recipes and Memories from Pakistan.* Frances Lincoln, London (2016).

Özlem Warren. *Özlem's Turkish Table: Recipes from my Homeland.* GB Publishing Org, Weybridge (2019).

Da-Hae West. *Eat Korean: Our Home Cooking and Street Food.* Mitchell Beazley, London (2016).

Kathy Willis and Carolyn Fry. *Plants from Roots to Riches.* John Murray, London in association with the Royal Botanic Gardens, Kew. (2014).

www.kew.org
Find out more about the scientific and horticultural work of the Royal Botanic Gardens, Kew.

Acknowledgements

As someone who has loved Kew Gardens since childhood, being asked to edit *The Kew Gardens Cookbook* has been a very special experience indeed. My thanks to Gina Fullerlove and Lydia White of Kew Publishing, for your enthusiasm, energy and expertise. It's been a real joy to work with you. Thank you, too, Hélèna Dove, Kew's kitchen gardener, for that very special tour of the kitchen garden – I now know what oca looks like!

Cookbooks are always collaborations and that's especially true in this case. My heartfelt thanks to our wonderful contributors who so kindly shared their delicious vegetarian recipes to help raise money for the Royal Botanic Gardens, Kew through sales of this cookbook. My collective noun for this group of chefs and food writers is 'a generosity'. Many thanks, too, to the publishers and agents who helped sort out permissions; your help was much appreciated.

Acclaimed food photographer Hugh Johnson brought his special magic touch to the food photography for this book. We are very grateful to you, Hugh. Huge thanks to accomplished food stylist Dagmar Vesely for all her hard work cooking such an array of recipes. She was ably assisted by Jo Linehan, Maddie Love and George Stocks. Many thanks, too, to prop stylist Tamsin Weston and photographic assistant Tom Teasdale and to Richard and Nicola of Warehouse Studios. It's worth noting, by the way, that all the food photographed for the book was eaten, rather than thrown away. As those of us who were on the shoot can testify, the recipes tasted delicious.

Jenny Linford

We have loved developing this book. Huge thanks go to the ever enthusiastic and tireless Jenny Linford for being a wonderful editor. We too would like to echo Jenny's thanks to Hugh Johnson; we learned so much and loved working with him, also to the incredible Dagmar Vesely and her team – Jo, Maddie and George – who skilfully cooked 40 delicious dishes, as well as to Tamsin, Tom, Richard and Nicola, named above.

The Kew Press office team have been greatly supportive of this project from the start; we would like to thank Sarah Farrell, Jo Maxwell, Seena Mistry, Heather McLeod, Ciara O'Sullivan, and particularly Tara Munday, who suggested Jenny Linford as a potential editor.

We hope readers will love the look and feel of the book they hold in their hands. We thank designer Ocky Murray for the enthusiasm and the fine result of his labours, also Guy Allen for his front cover illustration, and for putting up with the tweaking that got us there!

We are very grateful to busy Kew scientists who read and advised on the text; James Borrell, Chris Cockel, Aisyah Faruk, Melanie-Jayne Howes, Gwil Lewis, Mark Nesbitt, Tuula Niskanen, Tom Prescott and Paul Wilkin, and also to Hélèna Dove, Kew's kitchen gardener.

Heartfelt thanks go to the following: Michelle Payne for careful and thoughtful copyediting, as ever; David Segrue and Chris McLaren for their market wisdom and advice, Katie Read for all her press and media work, Jeff Eden and Ines Stuart-Davidson from Kew's Creative Services team for their help in sourcing stunning shots of Kew, and quote providers the BBC Natural History Unit, Ken Hom, Dan Saladino and Tim Spector.

And finally enormous thanks go to the 68 wonderful chefs and food writers who have literally made this book by contributing such an inspiring and enticing collection of recipes for us all to cook and enjoy – we are overwhelmed by your support of Kew.

Gina Fullerlove and Lydia White

Credits

Recipe credits

p. 126: Recipe from *Zoe's Ghana Kitchen* by Zoe Adjonyoh, published by Mitchell Beazley.

p. 89: Recipe from *Kew on a Plate with Raymond Blanc* by Raymond Blanc, published by Headline.

p. 120: Recipe from Vanessa Bolosier's *Sunshine Kitchen: Delicious Creole Recipes from the Heart of the Caribbean* (Pavilion Books).

p. 102: Felicity Cloake recipe first published in *The Guardian*.

p. 24: Recipe from *The Food of Sichuan* by Fuchsia Dunlop (Bloomsbury, £30), Photography © Yuki Sugiura.

p. 55: Recipe from *The Japanese Larder* by Luiz Hara, published by Jacqui Small.

p. 122: *Recipe from The Vegetarian Option: Simple, Vegetarian, Delicious* by Simon Hopkinson (Quadrille, ed. 2018).

p. 70: Recipe from *Eating for People, Pleasure & Planet* by Tom Hunt, published by Kyle Books (£26).

p. 158: Recipe from *The Green Roasting Tin* by Rukmini Iyer, published by Square Peg.

p. 176: Recipe extracted from *Sight Smell Touch Taste Sound – A New Way to Cook* by Sybil Kapoor (Pavilion Books).

p. 99: Recipe from *Food from Many Greek Kitchens* by Tessa Kiros (Murdoch Books).

p. 175: Recipe from *One: A Cook and Her Cupboard* by Florence Knight (Salt-Yard Books).

p. 69: Recipe from *Chetna's 30-Minute Indian: Quick and Easy Everyday Meals* by Chetna Makan, published by Mitchell Beazley.

p. 73: Recipe from *My Rendang Isn't Crispy and Other Favourite Malaysian Recipes* (2019) by Zaleha Kadir Olpin, published by Marshall Cavendish International (Asia) Pte Ltd.

p. 51: Recipe from *The Island Kitchen* cookbook by Selina Periampillai, published by Bloomsbury.

p. 84: Recipe from *Leaf* by Catherine Phipps, published by Quadrille.

p. 31: Recipe from *From the Veg Patch* by Kathy Slack, published by Ebury Press.

p. 170: Recipe from *East: 120 Vegan and Vegetarian Recipes from Bangalore to Beijing* by Meera Sodha, published by Fig Tree.

p. 59: Extracted from *Falastin: A Cookbook* by Sami Tamimi and Tara Wigley (Ebury Press, £27). Photography by Jenny Zarins.

p. 119: Recipe from *Home Cookery Year: Four Seasons, Over 200 Recipes for All Possible Occasions* by Claire Thomson, published by Quadrille.

Conversion tables

Abbreviations used in this book

g	gram
kg	kilogram
ml	millilitre
l	litre
mm	millimetre
cm	centimetre
tsp	teaspoon
tbsp	tablespoon

Weights

5g	¼ oz
15g	½ oz
20g	¾ oz
25g	1 oz
50g	2 oz
75g	3 oz
100g	4 oz
150g	5 oz
175g	6 oz
200g	7 oz
250g	8 oz
275g	9 oz
300g	10 oz
325g	11 oz
350g	12 oz
375g	13 oz
400g	14 oz
500g	1 lb
1kg	2 lb

US weight equivalents

25g	(1oz)	⅛ cup
50g	(2oz)	¼ cup
100g	(4oz)	½ cup
175g	(6oz)	¾ cup
250g	(8oz)	1 cup
500g	(1lb)	2 cups

Liquids / volumes

5ml	¼ fl oz*
15ml	½ fl oz
25ml	1 fl oz
45ml	1½ fl oz
50ml	2 fl oz
75ml	3 fl oz
100ml	3½ fl oz
125ml	4 fl oz
150ml	¼ pt
175ml	6 fl oz
200ml	7 fl oz
250ml	8 fl oz
275ml	9 fl oz
300ml	½ pt
350ml	12 fl oz
375ml	13 fl oz
400ml	14 fl oz
450ml	¾ pt
500ml	17 fl oz
600ml	1 pt
750ml	1¼ pt
900ml	1½ pt
1 litre	1¾ pt

*1 teaspoon

Measurements

5mm	¼ inch
1cm	½ inch
1.5cm	¾ inch
2.5cm	1 inch
5cm	2 inches
10cm	4 inches
15cm	6 inches
20cm	8 inches
25cm	10 inches
30cm	12 inches

Oven temperatures

140°C	275°F	gas mark 1
150°C	300°F	gas mark 2
170°C	325°F	gas mark 3
180°C	350°F	gas mark 4
190°C	375°F	gas mark 5
200°C	400°F	gas mark 6
220°C	425°F	gas mark 7
230°C	450°F	gas mark 8
240°C	475°F	gas mark 9

Index